THE ELEMENT GUIDE

SHYNESS

Lynne Crawford is a successful homeopath and Director of the London Shyness Centre. She also practises psychotherapy, hypnotherapy, NLP and bio-energetics. She has devoted her life to the study of personal development and has a particular interest in holistic therapies. She has trained and worked in both Britain and the United States.

Linda Taylor is a journalist. She spent several years abroad, working in Australia and South Africa, and returned to London in 1987. She has worked for several national newspapers including the *Guardian*, the *Independent* and the *Observer*. She studied English and Linguistics at Nottingham University and has a special interest in NLP.

THE ELEMENT GUIDE SERIES

The *Element Guide* series addresses important psychological and emotional issues in a clear, authoritative and straight-forward manner. The series is designed for all people who deal with these issues as everyday challenges. Each book explores the background, possible causes and symptoms where appropriate, and presents a comprehensive approach to coping with the situation. Each book also includes advice on self-help, as well as where – and when – to turn for qualified help. The books are objective and accessible, and lead the reader to a point where they can make informed decisions about where to go next.

In the same series

Addictions by Deirdre Boyd
Anorexia/Bulimia by Julia Buckroyd
Anxiety, Panic & Phobias by Elaine Sheehan
Bereavement by Ursula Markham
Childhood Trauma by Ursula Markham
Depression by Sue Breton
Stress by Rochelle Simmons

• THE ELEMENT GUIDE •

SHYNESS

Your Questions Answered

Lynne Crawford and Linda Taylor

ELEMENT
Shaftesbury, Dorset • Rockport, Massachusetts
Melbourne, Victoria

First published in Great Britain in 1997 by
Element Books Limited
Shaftesbury, Dorset SP7 8BP

Published in the USA in 1997 by
Element Books, Inc.
160 North Washington St, Boston MA02114

Published in Australia in 1997 by
Element Books
and distributed by Penguin Australia Ltd
487 Maroondah Highway, Ringwood, Victoria 3134

Cover design by Bridgewater Book Company
Design by Roger Lightfoot
Typeset by Footnote Graphics, Warminster, Wilts
Printed and bound in Great Britain by
Biddles Ltd, Guildford & King's Lynn

British Library Cataloguing in Publication
data available
Library of Congress Cataloging in Publication
data available

ISBN 1–86204–183–0

Note from the Publisher

Any information given in any book in the *Element Guide* series is not
intended to be taken as a replacement for medical advice. Any person
with a condition requiring medical attention should consult a qualified
medical practitioner or suitable therapist.

Contents

To Diana, Princess of Wales

Acknowledgements

This book is the culmination of a unique journey along a crystal path of learning and rich experience. I dedicate this book to my sister, Marjorie Ann Webb, Connie Preston, my family, Valerie Peppiatt, Kevin Kalkhoven, Peter Lekerman, Dr Ashken, Jane Alexander and those I love and cherish. Additionally my heartfelt thanks to my teachers, especially those who took the fear out of homeopathy, my teachers, nurturers and guides in my other disciplines, and above all Sathya Sai Baba.

Especially I would like to acknowledge the help I received from Paul de Vos, Grace Cheetham, Steve Andreas at NLP Comprehensive and Eileen Watkins Seymour and Clive Digby-Jones at the Ravenscroft Centre. Lastly, Sue Carter for her support and without whom this book might never have reached fruition.

Lynne Crawford

For John, who put the light in my life, and our daughter Sky, for whom the journey is just beginning.

Linda Jayne Taylor

When the sun rises and shines,
   not all the lotus buds
in the lakes and ponds bloom;
only those that are ready, do.
The rest have to bide their time.
But all are destined to bloom,
all have to fulfil that destiny.
There is no need to despair.

Sathiya Sai Baba

Introduction

The metamorphosis from being cripplingly shy to confident and comfortable in your own skin is achievable. Taking the first step and buying this book can empower you to change your future.

Shyness wreaks havoc in many people's lives. It is one of the most painful conditions you can live with and sufferers often do not seek help because of the fear and embarrassment of expressing what is wrong and talking about the problem. So it traps you in emotional pain and misery. You can spend a lifetime of under-achievement, loneliness, panic attacks and depression, unable to ask for help. This book will show you how to recognize the problem and then how to break the self-destructive pattern of shyness and begin to build a new life for yourself. This condition has not been fully recognized or acknowledged and has many causes, most of which will be outlined in this book.

Shyness is looking at oneself rather than at the other person. Feeling that people are hypercritical of you and that their undivided attention is focused on you. Shy people have a poor self-image.

You may have a false sense of what other people are thinking. Shy people frequently believe that people with whom they are interacting are focusing on their bad points. Socially, shy people may be embarrassed about certain mannerisms, their bodies or aspects of their character and they feel that the person they are speaking to is concentrating on that. Focusing on their perceived shortcomings, shy people ignore their strong points and by so doing, make failure more likely.

It can only take one bad event to make you a shy individual, but with incredibly far-reaching effects: it can limit you in your career, your relationships, your social life, in your ability to interact with other people, and can even mean that you feel too overwhelmed to go out, even to the shops. You may feel boring and uninteresting, that you have nothing to contribute to the conversation; you may fear that people will laugh at you. Apprehension about any social or work situation may take over and you may feel reluctant to take a position in which you may have to speak up and interact with other people, thus limiting your potential. You live in a paralysing state of fear. Shyness affects your ability to be yourself. You have no sense of your uniqueness. Instead, you worry about what others are thinking and you allow this to overwhelm you.

Shyness manifests itself in many ways. You may blush at the slightest occurrence in your life and become more and more mortified because you are showing a physical manifestation of your shyness to the world. The blushing becomes worse as you become more embroiled in the pain and embarrassment of what you perceive as an embarrassing physical symptom. You may suffer from palpitations, excessive sweating, impotence or frigidity.

The aim of this book is to peel away gradually the layers that are suppressing your inner self, the inner child, the real you. If you were able, as a toddler, to be aware of yourself within the universe as a whole person, then you are perfectly able to return to that state of well-being with work and with a growing sense of self-love.

Shyness is a powerful and limiting emotion which can lead to many physical illnesses. Our mind is connected to our body so our emotions will affect our state of health. Dr Bernie Siegler in his book *Love, Medicine and Miracles* states that those patients with cancer who believe that they have a right to live until they are 100 and enjoy life with a passion are exceptional patients and those 20 per cent generally survive cancer, even of the severest kind. Those with a lack of self-worth and with a belief system that they have no place on this planet just give up and die. It is useless, however, for a shy person to be told to pull himself together as that is unhelpful and probably the last thing you can do.

Crisis and confrontation are life-changing experiences that empower people to grow. The shy person will avoid crisis or confrontation for fear of how they might appear to other people whereas the non-shy person is not afraid to be open about their emotions, to show their vulnerability and to fail or be rejected. Emotionally you may feel totally crushed by past experiences and therefore avoid all areas of growth because you cannot handle the crisis in your life. Maybe your pain goes so deep and is so painful that it is impossible to cope with. Allowing yourself to get in touch with your pain of the past through the exercises in this book will bring about a confrontation of underlying traumas that will allow you to see why you are so scared.

The journey of self-healing can sometimes be painful but once you allow yourself to recognize why you have these self-limiting behaviours, a deeper inner understanding emerges and you then begin to love yourself and are thus empowered to go out and love others. Changing deep-rooted patterns of behaviour can take some time but the journey of self-discovery can unlock the inner beauty and the inner uniqueness that we all have.

The first battle, of course, is accepting that you have a problem. The second is finding a method of assessing and overcoming the problem. The difference between those who break the pattern of shyness and those who don't is in their attitude and their access to supportive therapeutic help. By combining your determination to overcome your shyness with our proven techniques, you will be able to take control of your life and live the life you've always longed for – along with the many other thousands of people who have overcome their shyness by using these principles.

Remember, it has taken years for you to be as shy as you

are. You probably devoted lots of time and effort to being how you are today! Re-programming the subconscious messages to your brain will be like building a house. It will take time but each success is another brick in the wall.

Rather like learning to play tennis, the best results are achieved if you concentrate on just one stroke at a time, achieving mastery over each one, slowly but surely building and developing. Taking the first step is always the hardest. But you have already done this by buying this book. Follow the exercises in this book and develop your emotional expertise and muscle. Keep practising until you develop healthy emotional muscles. Learn from each setback and don't beat up on yourself if it doesn't work immediately. Give yourself a break.

Learning how to break these destructive behavioural thought and speech patterns can radically transform your life, enabling you to become a more confident and skilled person, able to pursue your dreams and your goals. You are a unique, special human being. The problem is that at this moment you don't recognize this.

CHAPTER 1

The Causes

Shyness, that most crippling of emotions, may have one or many causes. Part of the therapeutic process is to pinpoint, if possible, how it started. Then exploring the problem will be possible and the healing process can begin. The process may take some time and thought but remember that it is part of the journey towards the confident and self-assured person that you can be.

The first thing to consider is when it all started. If you can, try to pinpoint when you were first affected by shyness. Follow it through in your mind from when it started, how it progressed and how much worse it has become. Pinpoint the fear. Were you always painfully shy as a child? Is this the state that you always remember being in? Or was it, perhaps, something that was triggered later in life? Do your parents remember you being in any way different after a certain event? If you can determine whether it is a behaviour pattern that has always been with you, or, instead, pinpoint the outset of your shyness, you can recognize the cause(s) of your shyness.

If you feel that you have always been shy, it may be due to one of the following reasons.

Family Patterns: Frequently we are moulded and shaped by our family pattern of behaviour. If your parents are nice people, who do not assert themselves, no doubt you will grow up to be one of life's doormats. Similarly, if your parents are highly critical – whether because they are criticized themselves and therefore automatically criticize you or because they are overly controlling or protective people who criticize you in order to keep you 'safe'– you will very quickly learn to criticize yourself and you will focus on yourself as an imperfect being, not worthy of being loved.

So, although you may come from a loving family, it is a negative force which shapes your behaviour and your view of the world. It is very difficult to overcome the effects of such faulty family input. If your parents told you 'you will never be any good at this' or 'don't bother with that, you know you will never get it right', you will usually think that.

One example of this is David who came to see me when he had just dropped out of university. He had always been nice and friendly, denying his right to be angry or say no. His father had sought to protect him with consistent criticism. Saying yes and denying himself was David's only defence. However, his repressed emotions became too much to bear. He panicked when he met people and spent his termtime in solitary confinement, only venturing out to lectures and tutorials, and eventually dropping out of university. Six months into treatment he has re-entered university and is beginning to make social contact. He is learning to be himself for the first time in his life and to find that people do accept him for himself. More importantly he is breaking through his rigid inability to feel any emotion at all. He is now feeling and expressing his emotions.

Shy Parents: Of course, we can simply 'learn' to be shy from our parents. Those who are very shy, very nervous and very inhibited usually impart this behaviour pattern to the family. We come out of the womb as confident beings but destructive conditioning can erase that confidence, especially if your parents lack self-esteem and a sense of self-love and self-worth.

If you feel that you only became shy after a particular time or event, it is likely to be due to one of the following.

Humiliation: This is a biggie. Did you suffer a childhood humiliation that has remained with you, conditioning your behaviour, colouring your responses, ever present in your mind, in your subconscious as well as your conscious, affecting your view of yourself within the world? There are many ways in which we can be humiliated and the shock can stay in our mind for life, unless we pinpoint and deal with it.

One of my patients, a blonde in her early twenties, whom we shall call Anne, was constantly humiliated at school. She was told that she was ugly by one child after another, and as a result believed it about herself. The abuse left her unable to judge her looks for herself, unable to recognize that the other kids were egging each other on, and that the remarks were simply a copycat response.

Years later she was still unable to form friendships and only went out with her mother. Looking into the mirror failed to dispel her belief that she was ugly. After a few sessions she began to recreate her perception of herself and to change the subconscious belief system she had built up to protect her from further humiliation and abuse. Now she is building a new life with enhanced confidence.

Trauma: Trauma comes in many forms and results in a subconscious conditioning that translates into unexplained behaviour and self-sabotage for the rest of our lives. The shock, grief and confusion which usually arise from traumatic events often programme our subconscious to avoid further pain – and the technique of avoidance all too frequently stays with us forever. Avoidance action is frequently quite inappropriate to situations that we have to face later in life.

Unexplained panic attacks and feelings of fear begin to emerge and prevent us carrying on our normal lives. Understanding the underlying cause can be the first step to overcoming this and taking control of our own brain.

The bereavement of a parent often triggers the problem. The grief of the other parent and the mismanaging by others of the child's neediness at the time can create misery and confusion. The child may have been sent to a friend, or shut out by the surviving parent as happened to Jane. She was sent to stay with a friend and an aunt told her of her father's death. Her only comfort was her friend who cuddled her to sleep. The day of the funeral, she went home and was surrounded by family, many of whom she hardly knew, and her mother wasn't there. Self-doubts and confusion over being left and excluded dogged her life. Recognizing why a partner's rejection and manipulative behaviour had destroyed her ability to make decisions about her future helped her to move on.

Bullying: The effects of bullying may stay with you for the rest of your life. Bullying can make you fearful of social and work situations. It may inhibit your studies, your work and your social life; fear of intimidation can destroy your self-esteem. One of my patients was afraid of going on holiday when she found that the older girls who had bullied her were going to be flying on the same aircraft. Fortunately, she voiced these fears and so we were able to deal with the problem. Another one of my patients was so bullied that she was unable to go to school for weeks on end. After a few sessions my patient was able to find the courage to return to school and to face the problem.

Put-downs: These put-downs may be from other kids, teachers, parents, friends, work colleagues, family members, spouses – whatever the source they constantly erode your self-esteem and your self-image. Sometimes we don't even recognize them. They can become a habit, a part of everyday life and are a core reason for our lack of self-esteem.

The unwanted child and those separated from parents at birth: It has been scientifically proven that even in the womb, babies are aware of what their parents are saying. Therefore, unwanted children and those who are subjected to parents arguing whilst in the womb will have an awareness from an early age. The anxiety of children who are surrounded by shouting and battling will remain in their subconscious for life.

In addition, children who are taken from their mothers at birth or delivered by Caesarian birth will also suffer from feelings of isolation and alienation. Encased inside an incubator, the babies cannot receive any comfort or succour from their mothers. These children may well spend the rest of their lives unable to understand why they cannot get close to people and have feelings of alienation and loneliness.

I was taken from my mother at birth as she was considered too ill to be able to pick me up or look after me. It was many years before I progressed to an understanding of how lonely I had been feeling. My mother had already lost her first child after it had been taken away from her because of her heart condition. She was not told that her baby was ill and dying, but, instead, first heard of her baby's death from the cleaner at the hospital. The trauma of having me taken away in much the same manner must have made her cut off completely. Whilst I was always loved there was certainly a difference in the way in which I was treated. Thus feelings of alienation and shyness were instilled in me at a very early age. I now understand why I was only able to love at a distance and found close loving relationships stifling.

Early experiences such as these remain in your subconscious but can be brought out through various self-help techniques which will be explained. Once you have an understanding of what is behind your behaviour patterns, then you can change these patterns.

The most important thing to do first, though, is to recognize that you are not alone. Amazingly enough, about 60 per cent of people are shy. Most of these shy people are either sitting at home, too scared to go out, or putting on a good front whilst dying inside. I know, I have been there. The good news is that with the help of this book you can jettison your shyness.

CHAPTER 2

The Feelings

Every one of us is taking a journey through life in which we learn to overcome certain problems. Life is growth. Overcoming the crippling emotional state of shyness can be a huge step in your journey, a step that can completely transform your life.

Many people put up a front to the rest of the world, concealing their innermost fears and feelings. In the worst cases these fears can stop you functioning properly; you certainly will not get the most out of your life. You deserve much more than that.

You may feel that the world's eyes are focused on you, ready to criticize your every word or action. You're deeply fearful of failure, of making a fool of yourself. In fact everyone is almost certainly too preoccupied with their own problems – and often their *own* shyness – to be concerned about you. You have to solve your own problems – and you can, easily. You just have to give yourself the chance and the will to do so.

You should already be patting yourself on the back: you have taken the first step today by purchasing this book. You've acknowledged that you have a problem and now, having done that, take the next step by working on this assessment chart. You will then have a measure by which to judge your progress. Decide whether you experience any of the following either often or fairly often.

POSITIVE SELF-IMAGE TEST

I am scared of saying no.
I always think I am wrong or to blame, rather than someone else.
It worries me whether or not others like me.
I feel I am not as important as other people.
I am scared of trying to make new friends in case they reject me and laugh at me.
I think other people are talking about me.
I am shy because I feel embarrassed in social situations.
I am self-conscious about my clothes and my looks.
I fear failure so much I won't try what my friends do, even though I want to.

Don't be disheartened after doing the test – you now have a clearer, more detailed picture of the problem and will be able to transform your life if you continue with the self-help therapies outlined later in this book. Self-knowledge combined with our easy, supportive techniques will enable you to be comfortable in situations you might have dreaded in the past.

Do you feel that nobody likes you or that they believe you are stupid every time you speak? For so many of us negative 'self-talk' comes as naturally as breathing – but these negative thought patterns reinforce your poor self-image and are destructive. Perhaps you look at yourself and make comments like 'If I lost 20lb then I wouldn't be so shy,' or 'If I joined a group of people they would find me boring.' Shy people often attribute their own beliefs to others. This is a critical factor – how we see ourselves is frequently very different from how the world sees us.

With this in mind try taking time to find out how the world does view you and then keep reinforcing that positive feedback to yourself. Concentrate on the good qualities by which the world actually judges you. Remember you're only telling yourself the truth.

Determination and staying power are a key building-block of your new life. When you learned to walk you didn't give up because you kept falling over, you just kept going until you could toddle, walk and later run. Overcoming your shyness and lack of self-esteem should be fun as well as immensely rewarding and your enjoyment will guide you to your goal of emotional mastery, which, in fact, is the cornerstone of a successful, happy life. Making a commitment to yourself to reach your goal, focusing on your goal and staying with the process until you get to where you want to be is how success is built in any area of life.

Do you suffer from unnecessary anticipation? Are you a 'what iffer?' Does every social or work event mean you slide automatically into a state of fear? Fear of breaking down under stress, of suddenly running away, of being unable to cope or even speak? All these are very genuine traumas which affect surprisingly large numbers of people.

In many cases feelings of shyness and lack of self-esteem can spring from insecurity about physical appearance. You may have been teased at school or by somebody cruel and thoughtless. The fact is *most* people don't like what they see when they look in the mirror first thing in the morning. However, the vast majority of us have all the qualities which we consider attractive in other people and on which we can focus in ourselves if only we'd give ourselves the chance to do so. Focusing on them will help you feel more attractive and lovable overall. In fact, it is often the little imperfections in a person that make them most attractive to the people who love them.

To begin that process, start focusing on the affectionate comments people have made to you. Start looking at couples you see in everyday life. You will notice that neither person is outstanding in every way. It is *you*, the intricate, kind, and very special you that people like. Stop focusing on what you perceive as your negative points, which are generally blown out of all proportion in your mind and hardly noticed by most people. Allow yourself to grow by focusing on those special attributes which make you unique and attractive to more people than you realize.

Do you focus on the few critical judgements people make to you instead of the many supportive and non-critical remarks?

Yes ☐   No ☐

Think about who you really are. List your strong points as well as your weak ones. Don't lie and be negative. If you have any doubts ask the people around you what *they* consider to be your best points – you will soon find you have a list! Focus on your strong points and view your perceived weaknesses constructively.

Being realistic about ourselves, taking on board the good points that others see in us as opposed to our own biased and negative self-image, can be the first step on the way to overcoming shyness. Telling yourself that you are a unique and special person can often be a self-fulfilling prophecy. If you genuinely believe it, it will be so.

You will find attitude plays a huge part in your success, both socially and professionally. Keep visualizing how good it is going to feel when you start dealing successfully with other people – keep that in mind and always endeavour to maintain a positive frame of mind. Remember, in football the world's top goal-scorers don't score a goal every time, they just try harder and aim for goal more often than most people. They often adopt a 'shoot on sight' policy – you could do the same. If you *do* more, and try to learn from what you're doing, you will definitely have more success.

Believe in yourself. Belief and will power recently built a hospital in southern India, which is acclaimed as one of the world's finest, in an astonishing five months from initial idea to the first surgical operation. All you have to do is believe you can – and then you will do it.

Confident, happy people have an air about them that is almost tangible. They attract people to them. They generally direct their thoughts outwards, ie, focusing on others instead of constantly dwelling on their own faults. Being genuinely interested in others will automatically attract people to you – as Dale Carnegie observed, it's the quickest and simplest way to make connections with other people. People who go into the community to help in charity projects and schemes, who radiate interest in their fellow man, always draw that same interest and love to themselves.

You can *train* yourself to be happy and confident. Shyness is just a habit, a form of negative emotional conditioning. It is within your power to shed this negative habit and become a person with high self-esteem. Acknowledging behaviour that has limited you in the past, and finding what you do well is what makes you special and unique.

A habit takes 21 days to establish: begin practising today to love yourself.

You may be a total perfectionist and take everything personally, feeling that maybe people expect too much, that you are unable to say no. You can't face a crowd. It is usually okay with one to one although sometimes you become tongue-tied, but crowds become a nightmare. You develop a very low opinion of yourself. You feel that people don't want to hear what you've got to say. You may find it very hard to build your own self-esteem. Panic attacks may result. This lack of self-esteem in men may cause sexual problems, leading to stress and impotence. The lack of self-esteem can make life especially difficult for men and the the trouble begins at an early age. Four times as many boys commit suicide as girls and more young men take their own lives now than at any time in recorded history. Whereas a girl will be more likely to express her lack of self-esteem through bulimia and talk to her friends about it, a boy will be unable to speak to his friends in the same way – he will not be able to offload his problems by talking about them, therefore alleviating some of the worst consequences. A boy may hide himself away at university and not speak to anybody and subsequently, after a large drinking bout, may attempt to commit suicide.

In fact, those people who attempt suicide rarely attempt it a second time – it is simply a cry for help and once counselling has been sought, often the need for another suicide attempt is alleviated. In your case, you must never let it get that far. Always seek help – talk to somebody, anybody – before sinking too deeply into feelings of worthlessness and depression. You will find it easier to rise out of it – you'll have unburdened yourself.

Remember, each small step that you take along the path towards self-esteem and self-acceptance will make you feel good about yourself. Sit down each time you have a success and congratulate yourself on it. The trick is to get moving and then it will quickly become a pleasure to *keep* moving. Use the assessment table below to help you every step of the way.

PROGRESS ASSESSMENT

1 What emotional goal or behaviour have you been working on for the past month?
2 Assess your success, your progress.
3 What have you learned from the process?
4 What can you do to improve your problematic areas?
5 Stay on track and continue to build on your successes and learn from your mistakes.

Recently, Scott M Peck, best-selling author of *The Road Less Travelled*, asked a group of people to write down what was most important in their life. The entire group scribbled furiously, some for half an hour, some for considerably less, and when Peck looked at their papers, he found that the people who were high achievers and who also had happy and balanced social, emotional and spiritual lives, had simply summed it up in one word: 'myself'. If you are unable to love yourself and to place yourself first you will always find excuses for under-achieving. You will never have *total* self-esteem but you can achieve a much higher level of esteem than you presently have. To consider this indulgent or selfish is to deny the fact that you are very important – if you do not consider yourself the most important person in your life, you will always lack self-esteem and will habitually self-sabotage.

To know that you are special, to know that you are lovable, most of all lovable by yourself, is the most important step you will ever take on a fantastic and essential journey. Confident people with high self-esteem are able to pursue their dreams and goals. Make a resolution now – it *will* be you. You can make it happen and be everything you want to be.

CHAPTER 3

The Therapies

Step 1: Half the battle is won – you've accepted that a problem exists. From now on you can begin to assert control over your shyness, rather than letting it control you.

Step 2: But recognizing there *is* a problem to solve is only half the battle. Only you know the real you, the person you want to be, the person you could be if only you weren't so shy. And this is where Step 2 comes in. It's this book! Reading it, and *using* it, can give you the knowledge and confidence to banish shyness from your life.

Many of my patients have one thing in common. They believe that others are focusing their undivided attention on them – and very critical attention at that. They have a belief system that says 'I am not perfect and people are being critical of me.' Perhaps it would be helpful for you to look at the popular people that you know and note that they are, in fact, considerably less than perfect. Just like you. Just like everyone.

Allowing yourself to access your feelings and inner experiences is truly enlightening. You will gradually learn to express your fears about not being very likeable and begin to create your own inner space, and space in your day, so that you can work out your own confusion and express your feelings. Write a diary in which you can express all your suppressed emotions, your anger and feelings of inadequacy. Perhaps discussing your problem with somebody whom you trust will help to restore your confidence. Writing a journal or using art as a therapy and acting out your role in the peace of your own room, or simply quietly meditating upon the problem, will help to bring all of these problems to the surface.

The exercises in the next chapter will help you and support you throughout this process. Perhaps you have been a victim all your life and you are now following a pattern – maybe fear is an issue, or feelings of inadequacy and a fear of rejection. Lack of self-esteem or lack of assertiveness may be a problem. You may act aggressively and then dislike yourself as a result.

Initially it is very important to restore confidence by learning to like yourself and recognizing that other people do like you. Focus on the people who are fond of you and try and establish why, what qualities you possess that they find appealing. Acknowledge your feelings of isolation and then make the commitment to go forward, no matter how many times you fall over.

It may take some time for you to feel confident about being assertive, doing the exercises and expressing your feelings, wants and needs. Do not expect a miracle to happen overnight. It won't. However, your confidence will grow as you develop your assertiveness skills and empower yourself to handle situations in a more appropriate manner. The self-exploration of the NLP skills that we teach you to banish negative thought and speech patterns will all help you make a dynamic change over the next few months. Remember that a toddler can only walk minute distances at first. Give yourself permission to take one step at a time, to stumble, to fall over, and to make mistakes, while striving always to pick yourself up and put yourself back on the path, never losing sight of your goal. Know that you *will* reach your goal and that no matter how many mistakes you make, by taking one small step every day, you will have progressed a long way by the end of the year.

Shy people have a major fear of rejection. There is a very negative thought process going on and sufferers tend to concentrate on themselves as opposed to others. You lack self-assurance. You don't take chances and won't risk embarrassment, feeling fundamentally uncomfortable with yourself and finding it hard to make an effort. You know you need to make an effort to get what you want but find it totally impossible. You avoid things you don't like and hide from a major part of life.

But as you begin to progress you will begin to feel more confident and become less sensitive to going out or to groups. You will be less self-conscious and not so worried about what people think about you. Once you begin to use your assertiveness skills, you will begin to feel a little more comfortable and a little more at ease. Each time you will handle a situation better. You will begin not to worry about things so much.

MIND–BODY BALANCE

Shyness, the crippling disease from which you are suffering, may not just be an emotional problem – frequently looking at the diet of a patient can help to eliminate this crippling state. Certain foods will, through absorption into the body, affect the mind. This is called the somapsychic connection – the mind and the body are interconnected via the endocrine system and certain foods will stimulate organs of your body which will, in turn, affect the brain.

Sugar, coffee, tea, carbonated drinks, foods containing colour and foods to which you may be allergic, as well as mercury in your teeth, have all been linked with mood changes, depression, agitation, anger and the physical symptoms of the fight or flight effect of shyness.

Food colourings, which are generally chemical in nature, are linked to behavioural problems, especially in children but certainly also in adults. Foods to which you are allergic may well not only be causing skin rashes to flare up, but if you take it to its logical conclusion, your internal cells will also be flaring up, even in the brain, thus causing you to exhibit aggressive or panicky behaviour. It would be well worth your while to have a test for food allergies to establish whether you are having an allergic reaction to anything.

Mercury fillings in the teeth have been found to be closely associated to mood swings and behavioural problems. Mercury poisoning can lead to aggressive and irrational behaviour. If you find your mood changes suddenly or you are constantly angry, then this may be part of the problem.

Sugar, lastly, is one of the most significant, and largely unrecognized, mood affecters in our society. It is responsible for chronic fatigue or depression, sadness, and for sharp mood swings and mood changes. Sugar in its commercial form is not a natural substance for the body and therefore should be removed from the diet as completely as possible. Try also to avoid sweetened drinks which are simply chemicals with sugar added. Our bodies do not have the necessary enzymes to assimilate chemicals and most of us are bombarded with over 300 chemicals a day.

Meat is extremely bad for your moods and along with sugar, colours and additives in food, can create tremendous emotional problems. It has a huge amount of adrenaline in it – when an animal is taken to an abattoir the adrenaline is pumping through its body, caused by the animal's fear and panic at suffering such a horrendous death. Eliminating meat from your diet will help to calm your adrenal system and has proven especially useful for people who suffer from fear and panic attacks.

To view the problem that you have as purely psychological and something that is your fault, is to be extremely harsh upon yourself – by eliminating harmful foods from your diet you can rid yourself of destructive emotions and help yourself to a calmer, more rational state.

We outline integrated self-help therapies that best suit your special needs. You can learn easy, supportive techniques that can be assimilated into your life, enabling you to be comfortable in situations you would have dreaded in the past. Learn to enhance your 'people skills' and overcome limiting beliefs, confidently establish rapport and communicate your own ideas.

FOCUSING ON OTHERS

As I mentioned earlier in the book, when you are in a conversation with another person, generally they are partially focused on what they are going to say next. Something that you have said will already have triggered a thought pattern in their mind. As people have 'monkey minds' and their thoughts flick from one thing to another, it is unusual for another person's attention to be totally focused on you. Whilst they may be looking at you they most certainly are not totally focused on everything about you and everything you say. One little exercise that I try with my patients is to ask them to touch their chin whilst I put my finger to my cheek. Interestingly enough, most of them put their finger to their cheek and it takes some minutes before they realize this. At any given time there is only a limited comprehension of what people see and what they hear. Judging yourself based on how you perceive others are seeing you is self-limiting. It is also pointless.

Whilst visiting the Sai Baba Ashram in India recently I realized there was very little shyness evident. There the emphasis is very much upon caring and loving your fellow man with much of your time spent in prayer and serving others. There is very little room for shyness because the devotees are very focused on finding their inner selves and caring for those around them. As a result, many of the devotees find that their emotional problems dissipate. Focusing on one's outer self as one believes the world sees it is bound to lead to problems; more focusing on the inner person and thinking of others helps alleviate shyness.

Shyness may spring from the fear of the unknown, the fear that the worst may happen, not the real situation, but simply deeply-embedded traumas which lead to fears and ingrained patterns. Sometimes you need just to let go and trust. You must have a little faith in people – you will often find that faith repaid handsomely. However, it is important to try to establish what has caused your original pattern of behaviour – if you think about it, what is the situation that springs to mind really strongly? Was there maybe a humiliation in school, a humiliation by another person? Was it severely critical parents or teachers? Somebody telling you that you couldn't achieve, that you weren't any good at something? These are self-fulfilling prophecies if you allow them to be. You cannot change the past but the present is yours and truly belongs to you, as does the future. You can make changes and completely redesign your life.

Perhaps you were taught to believe that you were always wrong. Alternatively some very cruel children in your past may have made you feel an outsider for some reason or another. Remembering a lot of the old hurts and pains, bringing them to the fore and examining them in an objective frame of mind will help you overcome this problem. Humiliations can go extremely deep, as can cruel behaviour patterns which have set this particular problem in motion for you. You need to have an awareness that your life is very special, it deserves working on, that you deserve to be treated as a unique and special individual – most importantly by yourself. What the world believes about you after that is never quite as important.

Establishing the source of your shyness is half the battle. It is important for you to figure out where the problem started, to start being logical about handling it and clear your past away for a brighter tomorrow. The next chapter will give you a number of practical exercises to do and it is important, during those exercises, to focus on where and how the problem started – precisely where and how the pattern began. That is the key to success. Remember, you only fail if you give up. No matter how difficult you may find it, keep trying and keep going and you *will* achieve a brighter tomorrow. Of course, tomorrow starts with today.

BELIEF TRANSFORMATIONS

Beliefs are frequently deeply embedded in our subconscious mind. They lead to self-destructive behaviour and limit your life. Perhaps you believe you are boring, have a large nose, are unattractive, or are simply a failure. Rest assured, for a start, that *everybody* feels like that at times. The exercise in the following chapter will show you how to do something about it.

CREATIVE VISUALIZATION

Creative visualization techniques are powerful tools for tackling many different kinds of problems. The main idea is to superimpose positive feelings over negative ones.

NLP

Neuro Linguistic Programming (NLP) is a dynamic form of psychotherapy as well as a powerful and empowering form of self-help therapy. The NLP exercises in the following chapter, which are simple and easy to use, can effect radical changes: they will help you to eliminate the fears and anger that may be controlling your subconscious; transform speech patterns that may be limiting your thoughts and body positions; and correct destructive thought patterns and belief systems. NLP teaches you to understand other people's operating systems, enabling you to relate better to the people you meet. You will learn to recognize whether people are visual, auditory, kinesthetic or touchy-feely people, and by recognizing these types you will learn to approach them on their level, thereby establishing a better rapport.

NLP also teaches you how to change your emotional state in a stressful situation. The use of programmed exercises will help you to transform a negative state into a positive one. An example of this might be hearing a love song many times with someone you love. The song will condition a good emotional state in your subconscious mind. Years later, when you hear it on the radio, the song will instantly evoke a rush of that pleasant emotion. In other words, you can run your own brain instead of your subconscious running you. As a child you emerged from the womb without fear or shyness. Having once been confident enough to assert yourself, it is life trauma and conditioning that have transformed you into a shy person. NLP can return you to the child you once were.

The Ravenscroft Approach is an approach to 'whole-making', the healing of a fragmented system. It is a model and a philosophy, a set of values and a process for a person wholeness. It provides a way of understanding how we protect ourselves by holding our energies, maintaining our splits, cut-offs, and it is a process for raising awareness, creating a new relationship with ourselves and, finally, fully integrating ourselves, so that we have released, taken back and are able to fully *be* and manifest our full power. It is a leading edge, a very powerful and fast-track way of both exploring and discovering, communicating with and re-creating, the whole self that we are meant to be.

BODY LANGUAGE

How you sit and how you stand is going to affect your mood and your actions. The body–mind connection is enormous. The exercise in the following chapter will show you how to alter your mood through posture.

CONVERSATION SKILLS

Consciousness is primarily expressed linguistically. Throughout the ages consciousness has developed and evolved in line with language. To use language in a purposeful way can influence your internal processes dramatically. The exercise in the next chapter will show you how to use language when speaking to other people.

STRESS RELIEF

Stress is the body's reaction to a dangerous situation. It is man's primeval fight or flight mechanism which helps you avoid danger. The adrenal system prepares the body to cope with perceived danger. Our modern-day lives are so stressful that our adrenal systems are often triggered simply by the pace of everyday living.

Stress-related emotions and panic attacks are a mind–body connection. When we are under undue pressure such as work-orientated deadlines or taking exams whilst carrying out our everyday tasks, we put our adrenal system into overload. We drink coffee and tea and take stimulants that all cause the adrenal system to pump out its chemicals. This causes a physical reaction that increases our fear or physical responses such as shaking and an awful feeling of foreboding.

Constant pressure on the adrenal system will eventually lead to stress-related diseases. Your immune system is put under considerable stress by this fight or flight response, often triggering physical manifestations of stress.

Probably in today's hectic culture the most stressful situations of all are the emotional and psychological pressures under which we are all placed from time to time. These are not a natural situation for the body. When you are stressed it makes normal functioning very difficult – you lose your clarity of thought and simple tasks can be much harder.

Stress will cause you to under-achieve in many ways. If you stress yourself you will begin to procrastinate and that can quickly add to your problems.

If you can focus on doing your best with everything you are doing without worrying whether people around you are doing better you will take a lot of the stress out of the situation. Stress will cause you to under-achieve in many ways. If you can just set out to achieve even your worst effort, put pen to paper no matter what and start, step by step, you will be amazed at how good your worst effort is whereas if you sit down and worry about the goal and how good it has to be then you are not actually going to be able to function properly. You are going to procrastinate, you won't sit down to start the job. What you will do instead is limit yourself. It is very difficult to do your best when you are stressed over the outcome, therefore you have to relax and enjoy the process.

Try to build on that by making a commitment to enjoy each day a little bit more. When you relax you become more inspired and efficient. Inspiration comes from within.

The exercises in the following chapter help you to define areas of stress in your life. Changing habits that lead to stress, ie, establishing what is important to your goals and desired outcomes, can help you overcome it.

ASSERTIVENESS

The core of assertiveness is being able to say what you want and what you need. Assertiveness is honouring yourself. People often develop non-assertive behaviour. We have many messages implanted in our minds as we grow up, as a result of family behavioural patterns or severe criticism as a child, such as 'children should be seen and not heard,' or, 'you are stupid, you don't know what you are saying.' We may be told that we should listen to our elders and that we do not know what we are talking about. These destructive behavioural patterns cause us to doubt our own ability to think and to have opinions. We lose our belief in our own inner knowledge. Severe criticism as a child can lead to a lack of belief in ourselves or our ability to make appropriate decisions or choices.

We are often severely criticized during our formative years and we automatically feel hurt when others criticize us. Learning to take criticism at its face value and learning from it is crucial to your growth. Criticism is not necessarily a criticism of yourself but of something you have done. There is a very distinct boundary between these two facts. The rush of adrenaline and the feelings we have block out all rationality; we take criticism personally and instead of being objective we are subjective. We try to defend ourselves when we should be seeking to rectify that which is not correct. Constructive criticism can be a very useful aid to learning. In fact, *everybody* has learned from it at one time or another. If we do not take it personally but see it simply as a learning process it will take the sting out of it.

Bear in mind that there is a huge difference between assertiveness and aggressiveness. Be very aware that assertiveness is very healing whereas aggressiveness will put the other person's back up. Non-assertiveness means that you deny your own rights, your own belief system. If you fail to express truthfully and honestly what you need and what you want, what your beliefs are, then you allow other people to trample all over you. Your ultimate goal is to avoid conflict but that outcome will simply lead to your being untrue to yourself. By establishing your own needs, beliefs and feelings honestly, openly and appropriately you will be able to progress – but remember you also have to respect others' feelings, needs and thoughts.

Aggressiveness is a violation of other people's needs, beliefs and rights. In essence, it is bullying and can frequently lead to the person getting her own way, but it is violation and it is inappropriate behaviour. Ultimately you will lose, emotionally and spiritually, whether you are the aggressor or the abused party.

Assertiveness is knowing what you want. What is appropriate for yourself, for the other person. You should check what is positive, feasible, within your control, basically what is correct for you and what you really want. Assertiveness is about communication with others, appropriate communication of your needs and your wants to others.

Assertiveness is giving a response to a situation that honours you and honours the other person. You have the right to judge your own behaviour, your own thoughts and emotions and to take responsibility for yourself. You have the right to excuse anything you do if you feel that it is appropriate. You have the right to decide if you are responsible for other people's problems or not. You have the right to change your mind and to make mistakes. That is the learning process in life. That is what this life's journey is all about. You also have the right to say that you don't know, you don't understand, or you don't care.

It is very easy to have ingrained belief systems that are quite destructive. Frequently people tend to sit back and not speak up. They want desperately to have what they want but they have no belief that they have any right to what they want. The remedy is to be more assertive and state your needs very simply, bottom line, without explaining yourself. Offer help by giving an alternative but if need be simply say 'No, I am not able to do this,' or 'Yes, I have a need.' This is very important. Sometimes people will be upset with you but if you explain yourself you will give them room to wheedle you round. Simply state 'No, that is not possible,' and never add '. . . because I have to do something else,' or '. . . because I do not wish to,' or '. . . because I am not allowed' for that will simply give people the leverage that they need to argue with you. A very simple and gracious 'No, that is not possible,' is all that is needed. A very simple 'I would like such and such to be done or to be given to me' is all you need to say. Sitting back and wishing for something will never make it happen. Progress and magic won't happen to you sitting in your room.

Confrontation when used assertively is not a pejorative description of the other person's behaviour. It is important in confrontation to point out to the other person what the long-term effects of their behaviour will be. You also need to point out what your feelings are about their stance and request more appropriate behaviour. By establishing what your needs, wants and rights are in your mind, perhaps even by writing them down, you then feel stronger about confronting people. You have a more appropriate idea of your rights and your needs and your wants and are then able to behave more assertively. Acknowledge the other person's good actions and endeavour to create agreement about their future behaviour. When you have elicited some form of agreement ensure that you keep mutual language going, i.e. we appear to have reached an agreement and I am very pleased about that. Or, I am so pleased that we were able to discuss this in such a constructive manner. If the other person stands there and refuses to speak or is not speaking to you, the best way to elicit a response is to say 'I have been talking for quite some time and you haven't responded in any way, could you please let me know your feelings on this matter.' Then have the courage to stop and be silent. They will at some point have to answer you and at that point you can go forward in your discussions.

Each step you take on this journey will be easier. Every time you exhibit assertive behaviour you grow in strength and courage. Assertive behaviour means stating the outcome you desire. It must be stated positively. It should be a feasible outcome, within the person's control. Specify the behaviour you require of the person, behaviour that will give you what you really want.

The broken record skill which assists you most in assertiveness is to keep repeating what you have said in the first place, ie, if a person asks you to do something you do not wish to do, you state 'No, I am sorry, that isn't possible.' If they persist and they keep asking and asking you simply repeat 'No, I am sorry, that isn't possible.' Eventually the message will get across that what they are saying isn't having an effect – and you have stayed true to your belief.

People may frequently try to manipulate you or criticize you unjustly. This is usually a very effective way of getting one's own way. It is helpful in this situation simply to acknowledge that some of what is said may be true but that you are going to remain true to what you have said and that you will judge your own actions appropriately. We all make mistakes and honouring our right to do that is very important. This style of criticism is not appropriate at any point and it can be pointed out that you have the right to make mistakes, that we learn and grow from our mistakes.

SELF-HYPNOSIS

Hypnosis comes from the Greek word 'hypnos' which means sleep. This is a state of consciousness close to sleep which still allows subconscious responses to be stimulated. By making powerful suggestions in your own words to your unconscious mind you can change behaviour patterns dramatically.

Self-hypnosis techniques are also extremely useful. Self-hypnosis is unlike the state of stage hypnosis with which we are all very familiar, which has brought hypnosis rather into disrepute. Self-hypnosis is a state of light trance, something which you may experience every day without realizing it. Frequently, when we drive along we can't remember how we have got from one point to another. This is a state of light trance or self-hypnosis. It's surprisingly easy to develop this into a mastery of self-hypnosis by the methods outlined in this book, but always remember when putting yourself into a trance to use your own words, your own phrases. Your subconscious will accept your own words far more easily than those of other people. In my surgery I elicit the subconscious needs of my patient first. You can do this for yourself, by relaxing or meditating and allowing the behaviour you wish to lose and the behaviour you wish to replace this with float into your mind. Just grab the first words that come to mind and work on them. Your subconscious knows better than your conscious mind what is required and what is important. By putting your own subconscious phraseology back into your mind you can achieve dramatic and lasting results. The subconscious mind has incredible power; if you allow this power to work, it can effect incredible changes in your life. You can be in complete control of your own subconscious and the most powerful and intricate resource you possess – your brain.

The power of self-hypnosis – which was probably first used, like many of the other therapies here, by the ancient Greeks, Egyptians and Chinese – can be incredibly simple because you are using your own words and are not allowing another person to have any power over you. I frequently use hypnosis as a technique in my practice, but only after eliciting the patient's own subconscious needs and phraseology. Then I simply repeat their own words back to them once they are in a hypnotic state.

Hypnotic language generally uses indirect commands. Gentle suggestions are far more effective than direct commands. Suggesting that the arm may feel light and may drift in the air is more powerful than suggesting to a patient that they may wish to lift their arm. Using a guided fantasy is also a way of inducing a hypnotic state. This is explained in Chapter 4.

It is important to input messages that will support your self and your self-development. Trying to remove personal responsibility will not work particularly well. You must aim for subtle change which will enrich and enhance your life. If you give the messages the chance to help you, they undoubtedly will.

Research has shown that post-hypnotic suggestions are particularly effective in treating strong behavioural patterns. For example, shyness, embarrassment and fear can prove particularly receptive to this form of therapy and healing.

CHAPTER 4

The Exercises

It is fundamentally important for you to gain mastery over your own emotions. You *can* change what you need to and be in control of your own emotions. You just need to take a few small steps and do some simple work until you find it becomes second nature to you. Knowing that your shyness has, until this point, controlled your life, you now need to recognize that you can rule your emotions instead of allowing your emotions to rule you.

EXERCISE 1 BELIEF TRANSFORMATIONS

Step 1
Take a sheet of paper and write down your limiting belief at the top of the sheet.

Step 2
List your emotions and fears arising from this limiting belief. For example, if you believe you are ugly and people laugh at you then you might write that you are scared of going out to meet people because they might laugh at you. You fear rejection and humiliation.

Step 3
How do you feel about the limiting belief now you have explored it more? Write down your feelings at some length – don't hold back.

Step 4
What would you like to change about your limiting belief?

Step 5
Finally, write what belief you choose to replace the old limiting belief system.

EXERCISE 2 THE MAGIC CIRCLE

The Magic Circle creative visualization technique allows you to take a situation or ordeal that is looming in your future and add new and empowering resources that will allow you to change your subconscious programming so that it never runs the same way again.

Step 1
Imagine an ordeal in the future you are dreading.

Step 2
Notice how you feel about it, how it looks and what you are saying to yourself to imagine it. Totally experience it and create a vivid picture in your mind. Ensure that the picture is in full colour, sound and intensity of sensation.

Step 3
Ask yourself what three resources or behaviours you would use that would support you in that situation. I need X ... I need Y ... I need Z ...

Step 4
Imagine a circle in front of you in a colour and size of your choice.

Step 5
Remember a time in the past when you were X. Totally experience that time in the past when you used that behaviour. When the feeling is strong step into your circle. Do the same for Y and Z.

Step 6
Bring to mind the ordeal you were dreading and notice the difference as you step into your circle. Is it lighter or darker, smaller or larger? Is it more difficult to recall the experience?

Step 7
Take your circle to another spot in the room and notice that you can take it with you anywhere.

EXERCISE 3 SWISH PATTERN

This is an extremely useful NLP exercise for changing your state and breaking destructive, emotional habits and behaviour, ie, feeling nervous and shy and lacking in confidence.

Step 1
First you need to identify the behaviour or the feeling that you choose to change. For example, when you feel shy and under-confident and are feeling really bad about yourself. Where or when would you wish to respond in a more appropriate fashion than you do now?

Step 2
Decide on a cue picture. This is what you actually see out of your own eyes before commencing the undesirable behaviour. It is important to ensure that this is an appropriate cue picture, as an inappropriate one may work but may do so at irrelevant times and places. It is helpful to associate as much unpleasantness with this picture as possible. Really experience the bad emotion that goes with this state.

Step 3
Create a picture of how you would see yourself if you had already made the desired change. Conjure up an image of how you would choose to be in your altered state. How would this enhance your self image? How would you feel

about yourself? Visualize yourself with an abundance of choices, the person you would be without your current limiting behaviour or response. Picture yourself having achieved the desired state change. This image needs to be without association. Be sure you are drawn to the dissociated image. If you aren't powerfully drawn to it, change it until it does.

Step 4
Place the cue picture from Step 2 on a movie screen, big and full of colour. See what you see out of your own eyes just as you are beginning to start the old undesirable behaviour.

Step 5
Place a small picture of the confident you, the you you want to be from Step 3 on the screen in the lower left-hand corner. Make it small and black-and-white.

Step 6
Now begin to swish the pictures. Allow the small picture to expand very rapidly to fill the entire screen. As it expands, it will become bright and multi-coloured, completely covering the cue picture. As the cue picture becomes covered, it will become small and dark.

Step 7
Open your eyes and clear your mind of the pictures. Shake yourself out.

Step 8
Repeat Steps 4 through 7 five times as rapidly as possible, remembering to stop and blank the screen each time you swish the pictures.

Step 9
Test by thinking of the cue picture and notice your response. The picture of the confident you should automatically

replace it. You may find that the first picture is hard to recall and maintain and that it is replaced automatically by the second picture of yourself as you wish to be.

Step 10
If the swish pattern has not realized a complete result, but only a partial one, review the steps to see where you need to modify what you did. Add whatever is necessary and repeat the exercise.

This exercise is adapted from Change Your Mind and Keep the Change *by Steve Andreas and Connirae Andreas © 1987 by Real People Press.*

EXERCISE 4 THE RAVENSCROFT APPROACH (HOLISTIC NLP)

This exercise came from a workshop entitled 'The Ravenscroft Experience' March 1994 © The Ravenscroft Centre.

The Ravenscroft Approach is a powerful holistic method of tapping into the subconscious mind. Frequently the answers we seek are hovering in the background ready to be tapped into if we just allow our minds to go blank so we can communicate with our subconscious. I have found this method to be extremely effective in my own practice. If you wish to follow this process it is advisable that you have somebody with you who is quiet and confident and can work with you through the exercise. You can do the exercise alone but it can be helpful to have somebody to help you through the process.

Step 1
Close your eyes and allow your mind to float. Thank every part of your body and your mind for doing a special job and also for protecting you.

Step 2
Allow a part of your body to float into your mind. Which-
ever part of your body first floats in, touch and communicate with it with your mind, touch and communicate
with it telepathically.

Step 3
Ask who or what is there. It may be a polar bear, a black
blob, a jellyfish, an uncle, an aunt, your mother, a friend,
or any object or being that is controlling that part of
your body.

Step 4
Ask what its intention is, ie, what is its purpose, its positive
intention by being there.

Step 5
After it has responded, ask whether it would rather be
doing something else, whether it would rather have its
freedom.

Step 6
If it says yes, thank whatever is there for being there, look
into its centre and through it, thank whatever layers you
may meet, and when you find the pure light hidden in its
depths, guide it back through and release it.

Step 7
The response to this may be 'no, not at the moment'. That
is OK but eventually, to eliminate the problem, you may
need to persist in looking into the depths of whatever is
controlling/holding that part of your body and allow it to
achieve its freedom.

The first time I carried out this exercise I tapped into my
subconscious and immediately visualized a polar bear on
an ice floe (floating) on an arctic sea. When I asked who it
was she said she was my mother and when I asked what
she was doing she said she was protecting me. When I

asked if she would prefer to be doing something else she said she would rather be running through the forest, feeling the grass under her feet and the sun on her back.

I almost immediately realized that as a baby I had been taken from my mother in the hospital and placed in the nursery. My mother was considered far too ill to hold me – she was forbidden to come down to see me and they only brought me up to see her once a day. Thus I was marooned in a sea of loneliness and very rapidly learned to laugh. My mother had told me that I had laughed all the time in the nursery and that I was bottle fed. In fact the nurses called me 'Snowball' because I had white hair and laughed a lot! The link with my subconscious empowered me to realize how isolated I must have been and how lonely. A baby normally doesn't learn to laugh until it is six weeks old – at that point I was being discharged from hospital, once again without my mother. Having learned to laugh well before six weeks must have been my own way of getting some attention in a lonely, solitary world.

I realized I must have received a great deal of attention when they bottle fed me which led to a pattern of eating problems as I grew up – basically because food equalled love and affection. I was also quite attention-seeking at times in my life, always a nice person and eager to please. This echoes my early experience of learning to laugh to please people and to gain attention when I was so desperately alone. It also made sense of the fact that every love of my life had always appeared to be on the other side of the world. I only understood love at a distance. I always felt somehow claustrophobic with a relationship close to home.

The Ravenscroft Approach was developed by Eileen Watkins Seymour and, latterly, by her partner in business and life, Clive Digby-Jones, of the Ravenscroft Centre in London, NW11 ORY. Together they consult with businesses, train executives, conduct private sessions and run workshops, giving people a chance to experience for themselves an approach that must be tried to be believed.

EXERCISE 5 BODY LANGUAGE

Simply looking up when you feel depressed will alter the serotonin flow to the brain and will chemically alter your mood, as will a smile. Have you ever noticed how difficult it is to feel depressed if you are walking briskly, looking up at the sky and smiling?

Shy people usually hang their heads and look at the floor, trying to hide, hoping people won't notice them. Nothing can be more self-destructive. Taoists say that 'When you are depressed, go fly a kite.' If you notice people who are confident, they are standing up, they are looking up, they are bright and they are breezy. Whenever you feel fear coming on and you feel that you want to sink into the background, just do one thing – smile. Again and again I notice with patients in my surgery that when they are depressed and are talking about their shyness, they sit there with their shoulders hunched and their heads down. I ask them to look up, make them aware of their body position so that whenever they feel fear, anguish and shyness coming on, they can use techniques to change their negative state into a positive one.

Body position is also important if you are going to a social event, a party etc. If you sit in the corner wishing you weren't there it is going to show in the way you position your body. It is important for you to be aware that if you sit back and smile and look inviting, then people will want to talk to you.

Your body language at work can also be very telling. If you sit there chewing your pencil, looking worried, hunching your shoulders, people are going to feel that you are not doing your job properly. In contrast, looking self-assured and confident can make all the difference to your career progress. If you have a fear of speaking on the telephone or you feel that your voice isn't coming out properly and you wish to sound confident when you call people, you could try standing up while speaking. It does come across in your voice and it makes you sound very powerful and very confident. Always try to smile when you answer the phone – once you have developed this habit your smile will come through at the other end of the line and make you far more approachable. Remember that leaning forward will also affect your voice, just as sitting back will make you look relaxed and sound relaxed. It also alters your mood.

Perhaps a chat with somebody who is popular might be helpful. You might ask them how they think other people feel about them. That would help you replace your perception of what other people think of you with a more accurate view of what they *really* are thinking about you, thus enabling you to break much of the shyness pattern.

EXERCISE 6 FIVE-STEP CONVERSATION SKILLS

Step 1
Don't ask closed questions, they are bound to result in yes or no answers and do little to further a conversation.
Examples:
'What is your job?'
'How old are you?'

Step 2
Ask open questions that elicit more information and invite conversation.
Examples:
'How do you feel about your job?' or
'How do you feel about this situation?'

Step 3
In conversation do only two things: request or make a statement.

Step 4
Listen to what the other person is saying instead of your own inner dialogue; you will probably find something in what they are saying to prompt further conversations.

Step 5
Try to find something you have in common with the other person and then you will have something to talk about.

STRESS RELIEF

Stress will cause you to under-achieve and procrastinate. Simply trying to make yourself reach a perfectionist goal will not be helpful because, after all, nobody is perfect! Instead, you need to look at your stress levels and work on ways to reduce them.

EXERCISE 7 DEFINING AREAS OF STRESS

Define what are the most stressful areas of your life. Analyse what is causing the problem. Is it a particular person or situation or your personal restrictions?

Being completely honest with yourself answer the following:

The problem areas are:

1 ....
2 ....
3 ....
4 ....

Having established this, now analyse what you need to do more of to eliminate these stressful areas.

- I need to .... some more.
- I need to .... soon.
- I need to .... sometimes.

Taking your responses and analysing them you can identify:

- changes you would choose to make;
- what you want to retain;
- future goals;
- areas which need more flexibility.

EXERCISE 8 CHANGING HABITS

Frequently stress is the result of unchallenged and negative habits developed through many difficult situations. By analysing our stress habits we are consciously beginning to make different choices. Gaining mastery over our habits and choosing to change them relieves stress dramatically.

Step 1
Be flexible in your thinking and attitudes.

Step 2
Establish goals: personal – relationship – career – family.

Step 3
Establish your boundaries: personal – relationships – career – family.

Step 4
Having established your goals and boundaries don't waste energy on non-essential and non-productive time bandits.

Step 5
Establish your list of resources for handling stress as well as the negative resources that damage you. These resources could be people, activities or pools of knowledge.
   a) Eliminate negative resources.
   b) Find creative ways of enlarging positive resources.

ASSERTIVENESS

When faced with stressful situations in your life, stop for a moment and take time to ask yourself:

- what am I feeling?
- what am I thinking?
- what do I want?

Remember that you have rights and take the time to define those rights before you go any further. These rights are:

- to be happy;
- to be loved;
- to be valued;
- to have a sense of self-worth;
- to have a sense of self-love;
- not to be abused;
- to be happy;
- to be responsible for your mistakes;
- not to accept responsibility for the mistakes of others.

Assertiveness is about taking responsibility for your actions. Establish your boundaries. Know the end result that you want out of a situation. Most people go into situations without preparation and without forethought. This is their stumbling-block. This leaves them feeling inadequate and unable to cope. Without knowing your required outcome you end up feeling guilty if you say no. You also lose if you give way, and end up wishing you had stood your ground and achieved your objective. This undermines your self-esteem still further which increases your shyness. It's a vicious circle.

Choosing to reach a solution with someone with whom you may be arguing takes skill and practice – and we're not generally taught how to do that. This skill does not come naturally; most assertive people have been taught assertiveness skills. The simple fact of knowing what you want out of a situation and what you want from the other person could stop you feeling even more lacking in self-esteem, and make you feel good about yourself, increasing your own sense of self-worth.

EXERCISE 9 RESULT OUTCOMES

ME	——————————————————	OTHER

What do I want for me?

....
....
....
....
....
....
....
....
....

CHECK ————————→

| Positive |
| Feasible |
| Within control |
| Appropriate for both of us |
| Really want? |

EXERCISE 10 HANDLING NO

Knowing when to say 'no' is absolutely fundamental to increasing your self-esteem. Handling NO needs a structured approach. We are not taught this skill as children and many of us never acquire the knowledge or methodology throughout our lives. Establishing fair and appropriate boundaries and outcomes prior to any confrontation will support you emotionally. Give yourself the gift of praise when you do well and analyse without blame if you fail. Above all, learn from the experience.

Step 1 – Goals
Firstly, set out your goals:

- confidence
- motivation
- self-esteem
- determination
- self-worth
- renewed compassion for others as well as yourself
- add your own goals here.

....
....
....
....
....

Step 2 – The Problem
Define the problem (as questions).

'Why?' .... 'Where?' ....

Determine what the issue is, and then gather complete and comprehensive information on it.

Step 3 – Identify Your Negative Feelings
Are you:

- angry?
- hurt?
- unsure?
- scared?

Step 4 – Importance
Establish priorities, personal boundaries and needs:

- How important is the issue?
- What do I stand to lose if I buckle under and say yes?
- What are my needs?
- What are the consequences of my not having my needs met?

- What would I be comfortable with?
- What is the bottom line for me?

Step 5 – Options
Establish alternatives and options that would be appropriate for both.
What else can I suggest as an acceptable alternative?

1 ....
2 ....
3 ....
4 ....

Step 6 – Delay
- Decide never to give an ill considered answer.
- Create a habit **now always** to say, 'I will think about it and get back to you.' This enables you to go away, think rationally and go back with a well-formed answer on your ground. This empowers you and avoids hasty and inappropriate responses. It also stops you from being pressured unscrupulously by other people. Never say 'yes' or 'no' immediately.

Step 7 – Decide and Take Action
This is done during the delay process above.

- Evaluate your options and choose the most appropriate one with a well-formed outcome.
- Take action and communicate it to the other person as soon as possible.

Step 8 – Leave the Door Open
Should the other person try to force you to change your mind, resolutely repeat your bottom line and add 'if you change your mind . . . '

This leaves the door open for the other person to accept your decision.

Step 9 – Honouring Your Needs
- Remember you have the right to make your wants and needs known to others.
- When you do not ask for what you want, you deny your own importance.

Step 10 – Practise saying 'No'
Clearly and directly without apology or justification. Simply state your feelings and your needs. Do not argue with what you have stated. Do not explain, simply state that the bottom line is that this is not possible. This way you can avoid giving leverage to the other person who may be trying to force you to do something you do not wish to do.

Once you have established your bottom line, do not explain yourself or be aggressive. Simply repeat firmly what you have said. Do not become angry – that will weaken your position.

EXERCISE 11

Most people are crushed by criticism or by the word 'no'. Research shows that people who handle criticism well do so because they see it as a learning process, not as a destructive process.

Ask yourself:

- was this correct?
- what have I learned from this?
- how can I improve on this in future?
- how can I create positive feelings about the situation?

ASSERTIVENESS – DOS AND DON'TS

DO	DON'T
1 Request action . . . 'Will you?'	Ask with 'Why don't you . . .?' 'Could you?' 'Can you?' 'Would you?'

2	Use clear, appropriate directives	Expect others to d without a request 'I need . . .'
3	Stand your ground by calmly repeating	Use 'you' with neg
4	Add power with eye contact and firm tones	Say 'It occurred to me' or 'you know', 'maybe. . .'
5	Express feelings: 'I'm angry about . . .'	Say 'You make me . . .' feelings.
6	'No, thank you'	Label behaviour or judge attitude
7	Use 'you' followed by fact	Become aggressive or give in
8	Say 'I think . . . thoughts'	Threaten or use exaggerated language
9	Say 'I feel . . . mad, sad, glad, scared'	Accuse – 'You never (always) . . . !'
10	Give examples of unwanted behaviour	'I can't', or 'I am unable to'

SELF-HYPNOSIS

EXERCISE 12 A Guided Fantasy

There are many myths surrounding hypnosis. Because of the popularity of stage hypnosis, people feel that they will fall into a deep sleep and do stupid things whilst in a hypnotic state. This is not a true therapeutic state and you do not have to be asleep to benefit from hypnosis. Ideally, hypnosis or self-hypnosis as a therapeutic treatment will lull you into a relaxed and semi-trancelike state. By semi-trancelike I mean the sort of state that you go into when you are driving your car and you don't remember the sequence of actions that have brought you to a certain place. Or the sort of state that you go into when you are speaking to somebody with a boring and monotonous voice and you lose track of what they are saying.

A very simple way of putting yourself into a trancelike state is to make a tape. Speak very slowly in a very low and modulated voice and use the word 'and' continually. If you tell yourself on your tape to relax more and more and more, using the word 'and' every few words, you will place yourself in an appropriate state to receive the information that your subconscious feels is appropriate.

Start the tape with a guided fantasy. Take yourself on your favourite country walk or visualize yourself walking along a warm Caribbean beach, wherever you would most like to be walking. Talk yourself through it, talk about the things that interest you most, the sound of the sea or the beauty of the flowers. Tell yourself about a waterfall with a rainbow above it, or talk to yourself about any beautiful sight you would wish to see. Put in some thought before you start and then just close your eyes and talk slowly and quietly into the tape. This is called a 'guided fantasy' and as you relax you will sink deeper and deeper into a trancelike and totally receptive state which will allow you to eliminate the behaviours you wish to lose and to input the new, empowering behaviours that you wish to gain. These are the behaviours you defined in Exercise 1 of this chapter.

It must always be remembered that hypnosis is a very powerful tool and it should not be played with, used for amusement or to manipulate others. Hypnosis can backfire if used unethically.

By making your personal self-hypnosis tape you are tapping into a powerful way of inputting positive thoughts and behaviours into your mind. Simply play some soothing music with the sound of dolphins or tinkling bells or flute music. Play it slowly and quietly in the background.

Then start off with your notes from Exercise 1 which will show you the negative behaviour that you wish to lose and the positive behaviours your subconscious feels are appropriate to substitute for the negative behaviour. Throughout the tape suggest the erasure of your negative behaviour and the adoption of the positive behaviours.

Then develop your guided fantasy addressing yourself in the second person, using your own subconscious phraseology gleaned in the reframing exercise above. For example, you could say 'the lack of confidence and shyness is slowly slipping away where it is left in the footprints in the damp sand behind you. The waves gently erase the footprints so the negative emotions drift out to sea. And as you walk you gather up the positive emotions of enhanced self-esteem and confidence and each step you take increases these new and supportive emotions.'

When you have made the tape, play it frequently to yourself when you have time to relax or before you go to sleep. I suggest that, at the end of the tape, you make a statement which enables you, if it is appropriate, to return to the here and now. Say that if it is not appropriate, however, you will sink deeper and deeper into a deep and refreshing sleep. This allows you to sleep if you want to but then, if you have to, to get up and do something after your self-hypnosis session. Do not worry that you will never wake up from this exercise. Your subconscious will wake you when it is appropriate.

A Simple Guided Fantasy

As you are walking along a white sandy beach, you can feel the heat of the sand under your feet and the grains of sand slipping between your toes. You reach the damp sand by the edge of the sea and you can feel the coolness of the sand under your feet and you can see it is a deeper colour, and if you keep walking along you can hear seagulls crying up above you and the sound of the waves as they reach up onto the beach, and you can feel the small bubbles of the water as it breaks upon the shore and each wave washes the sand up and you can feel the gentle rush of water over your feet. And as you walk further you sink deeper and deeper into a state of total relaxation and you feel totally at peace with your world. And as you keep walking along you notice the turquoise of the sea on the far horizon and you see it merging with the deep blue, clear sky above, and as you sink deeper and deeper into a state of relaxation you can see a small boat on the horizon with its white sail bobbing up and down with a lone fisherman casting his net, and as you watch it going up and down, up and down with each wave, you sink deeper and deeper into a state of total relaxation and you feel the cool of the water against your ankles and the firmness of the sand under your toes and you look down into the clear water and you see small fishes darting in and out in the clear water just beyond the waves as they break upon the beach and each step that you take you sink deeper and deeper into a state of total relaxation. And as you keep walking along, sinking deeper and deeper into a state of total relaxation, you notice that the negative feeling and belief (this is where you state the belief that your subconscious has identified as a behaviour you choose to lose) slipping, being left in the footsteps behind you in the damp sand and you allow all of the negative feelings to slip away behind you, and as you keep walking along sinking deeper and deeper into a state of total relaxation you gather to you the positive belief (here you use the words that your subconscious used to you in the reframing exercise as positive behaviours that your subconscious chooses to use in place of the negative behaviour) which will empower you to grow and develop and become more and more secure and more and more relaxed, more confident than ever before.

Continue with this. Remember and record your journey along the beach, noticing that you are leaving the negative behaviour behind and gathering to you the new positive behaviours that your subconscious would wish to substitute for the negative behaviour. Notice anything that springs to mind that would appeal and then turn around on your journey and begin to retrace your steps. As you walk along notice that the waves have washed the negative feelings out to sea and keep gathering new positive beliefs. If you return to the place from where you started you will notice that you feel more calm and more confident and more relaxed. Tell yourself that each time you play the tape the negative feelings will drift further and further out to sea and that your positive behaviours will become more powerful each time you listen to the tape.

Play this tape to yourself as frequently as possible. Don't stop once you have achieved the effect as you will need to reinforce your reconditioning. In the same way that if you stop going to the gym you become flabby, your mind can easily forget its reconditioning. Every now and then, therefore, go back to the exercise, repeat it several times and get yourself back into peak condition.

CHAPTER 5

The Situations

We all know, to some degree, the fear of going into a strange place, but for the shy person this is an intolerable ordeal. To mix socially or to fulfil oneself in one's job can become impossible as a result of such deeply ingrained and self-limiting beliefs. Acute self-consciousness can severely handicap and disempower sufferers, making it impossible for them to fight their fears and face new or challenging situations.

Any social interaction, even one so mundane as a trip to the supermarket, can mean a potentially embarrassing or frightening situation for the shy person. Fear of looking foolish or people thinking you are stupid becomes an all-consuming conviction. Everyday situations that the average person doesn't think twice about become potentially embarrassing situations or, at worst, almost impossible ordeals.

Our aim is to help people conquer this debilitating and devastating condition, an affliction which can affect people from every walk of life, from housewives to accountants, from businessmen to students, who may go through an entire degree course without any social interaction whatsoever. No one is exempt from this debilitating and devastating state of mind and, in the past, many have spent their lives unable to conquer it. But it *can* be cured.

Stress-related emotions and panic attacks are a mind–body connection, our adrenal systems often being triggered simply by the pace of everyday living. Excess pressure, such as deadlines and examinations, can put our adrenal system into overload. Constant pressure on the adrenal system will eventually lead to stress-related diseases. Stress can also lead you to under-achieve in many ways. Taking time out to reduce stress can prove very rewarding for you. Apart from stress-relieving exercises one very important thing that you can do, which I was taught by Dr Neil Fiore, is to stop focusing on the goal, on winning, and start focusing on your personal best. If you can focus on doing your best, without worrying whether people around you are doing better, you will take much of the stress out of the situation.

MEETINGS AT WORK

The work situation is a fraught one for the shy person. Meetings are a nightmare! Fearful that someone may be looking at you in case you say something wrong or stupid, your mind goes blank; you want to run out of the room but you can't. At any moment you may be thrust into the limelight, fulfilling your worst fears that you don't know your subject and could be made to look a fool. You fear that someone may bounce something off you and make you look an idiot in front of your boss.

First you need to prepare and to know your subject as well as possible. If called upon to stand up to speak, pause a few moments. If possible, have prepared notes at hand to prompt you. Take time to notice how many other people in the room are also nervous when they speak. That way you will know that you are not alone. In fact, you are certainly *not* alone, even amongst people who earn their *living* doing this – even top actors, comedians, opera stars and pop stars feel extremely nervous before they go on the stage.

You might also consider joining an excellent organization called 'Toastmasters', a group which takes nervous and shy people and teaches them the various techniques of public speaking. The members, who themselves know what it is to have been nervous in the past, run a well-structured programme which will enable you to overcome your fears of standing up and holding forth in front of other people and, indeed, help you even to *enjoy* it.

Before you go into any meeting use some of the homeopathic or flower remedies mentioned at the end of this chapter, as well as employing some of the techniques. In time you could even be winning prizes for public speaking! You're as capable as anyone else of doing it well.

Shy people often have one major fear, that is the fear of rejection, a fear that has often been with them their entire lives. They blush, they dry up. They are OK when they are in their comfort zone but if they take one step outside they go to pieces. They become very quiet and go into a panic before they speak. In some cases stress is unavoidable, but lack of self-confidence is holding them back in every area of their life. With a little work and self-belief, the benefits they could enjoy would be immense.

There is a very negative thought process going on here and the sufferer tends to concentrate on their own fears as opposed to, say, the personal interests of the people around and in front of them. They go full pelt into a negative thought process, never thinking that the other person might be thinking good things about them. They don't take chances and they won't risk embarrassment, feeling fundamentally uncomfortable with themselves and finding it hard to make an effort. They know they need to make an effort to get what they want but find it totally impossible. They become very successful at avoiding things they don't like and hide from a major part of life. They may even be perfectionists, focusing critically on themselves instead of others.

If you recognize any of these traits, rest assured you *can* change them. In fact you can change *everything* in your life and you should relish and enjoy the power you have to do that.

As you begin to progress you will begin to feel more confident, becoming less concerned about going out or in groups of other people. You will feel less self-conscious and not so worried about what other people think about you. You will begin to use your assertiveness skills and whilst you may still avoid certain social situations, you will begin to feel a little more comfortable, a little more at ease.

You may still be quiet at meetings, but now you can handle that – sometimes it is OK. Gradually you begin to progress and build little blocks – after all, a house isn't built in one fell swoop, it is build upon foundations and bricks added one by one, floor upon floor. This is how you progress. Each time you handle a situation a little better until it holds no more terrors for you. You build a stronger building. You begin not to worry about things so much – because, after all, 95 per cent of the things you worry about never happen and those that do prove surprisingly easy to handle. Remember – almost every problem can be solved with energy and imagination.

One major problem with shy people is that their attention span is often not very good. You may lose the thread of what the other person is saying. They may have a vaguely hypnotic voice and send you into a sort of trance, or you may be so busy panicking inside that you can't concentrate on their words. One very good trick for handling this is to stop and say 'I'm sorry, I'm not quite clear on what you just said, would you mind clarifying your point?' This gives you thinking time and allows you to bring your attention back on course, by which stage you should be able to think of an appropriate answer. Never be afraid of slowing things down, if necessary, to your speed. That can help you impose yourself on situations, rather than letting them control you.

For any business situation it is also sometimes helpful to have a formula as to how to make healthy and appropriate decisions. The following is a format for appropriate decision-making that may be useful.

DECISION-MAKING PROCESS

- Define the problem.
- Gather information.

- Look at alternatives.
- Define possible consequences of your action.
- Identify any pressures, ie, deadlines/boundaries/ restrictions.
- Is it appropriate? Consistent with who I am and what I believe? Is it compatible with my needs and those of others?

JOB INTERVIEWS

Numerous shy people never reach their full potential because of their inability to face job interviews – the paralysis of shyness takes hold and careers and personal growth can be stunted. To combat this, first take on board the complimentary things that are said about you in your present job and repeat these remarks to yourself. Keep telling yourself that you're a very good candidate for the new job. Then prepare yourself for the interview, both psychologically and practically. Firstly, you need to show your excitement about yourself – when you're excited about yourself it is infectious. Secondly, show your eagerness about the company to which you're applying and their product. You'll probably have to do some homework about this to enable you to speak knowledgeably at the interview. Before the interview look at the advertisement for the job and highlight the key words – then use these key words in your conversation with the interviewer. Keep using some of those words, thereby repeating their own words back to them. This creates an association – that you are just like them. You're literally 'talking the same language'.

Additionally, you may find it useful to phone the interviewer or the personnel department and find out what qualities they are looking for in the applicant, as well as to get a picture of their company culture. Find out as much information about the company as possible prior to the interview. Your work plays a major role in your life – on average, you will spend up to one-third of your life working – therefore it is vitally important that you spend a little time preparing for an interview that could have such a major effect on your life.

Then 'case' the company: try to pop along to see it before the interview. That way you will know where you are going, so you can plan your journey to give you time to spare and you know what clothes are worn. This will give you a head start. Do not go dressed inappropriately – 87 per cent of their initial, and often lasting, view of you will be based on their first impressions. Be prepared and do your homework.

Should you fail to get the job that you applied for, don't be disheartened. Phone the personnel department and ask them to give you some feedback, hopefully constructive criticism, as to why you failed to secure the position. Don't avoid doing this because you think they won't have time to tell you – in fact, very few people ask for feedback of this sort and it can be extremely valuable. It can even prove to be the difference between your dream job and no job at all. If necessary be a 'pleasant nuisance' – by being polite and charming you can find out a great deal of inside information which could prove very useful to you. Change your perception from that of failure to *learner* – you're on a learning curve, establishing why you didn't get the job and using the information received to make your next application more powerful and more successful. Each 'no' takes you closer to a 'yes'.

Don't put all your eggs in one basket. Apply for several jobs. This will give you plenty of experience and make you feel more comfortable at each interview as you become comfortable and confident with what you have to do. Successful people are not necessarily successful at their first attempt, they simply have more staying power and keep trying.

As Tim Bevan, the British producer of such award-winning cinema blockbusters as *Four Weddings and a Funeral* and *Fargo*, said when he was asked why he was more successful than most of his peers, 'Because I've been *rejected* more than them too.' If it happens to you, don't get disheartened – you're not just in good company, you're in the *best* company.

WORKPLACE

There are many people out there who are treated like doormats in the workplace, frightened to complain, often working under bullying and abusive management. These people are scared for their jobs, and too frightened to make a move. Frightening as a move may be, it is frequently the answer to many of your problems. Don't sit there in paralysed fear and agony. Get out into the marketplace and try different jobs. See what is available through agencies. Alternatively, try to obtain a different position in your current company.

Some jobs are soul-destroying. You may find yourself being treated like a conveyor belt, being given massive amounts of work. A quick comparison with other people's workloads will tell you if yours is acceptable or not – if it isn't, say something or *choose* to change your situation. Other sections of this book will tell you what to do in such circumstances.

RELATIONSHIPS

Frequently the shy person doesn't go out, doesn't form relationships and sinks into a world of loneliness and self-depreciation. To them, relationships frequently lie beyond the realms of possibility. Frequently the shy person feels that people are attacking him or her and defensive feelings arise.

Relationships frequently fail to happen because a first meeting is so painful and difficult for the sufferer that the other person finds them completely impossible to get on with, totally uncommunicative and downright hard work. The other person frequently feels uncomfortable in the presence of the chronically shy and having to make all the conversation becomes extremely wearing.

When the shy person *does* manage to form a relationship they frequently spend a lot of time avoiding difficult or potentially embarrassing situations – the fear of humiliation restricts the shy person's natural desire to go and try new things. The crippling effect of shyness can also lead to tragic breakdowns in relationships. Frequently, the sufferer is just told to go out and face up to the problem and, of course, this is no help whatsoever. The shy person might avoid meeting their partner's relations or avoid going to crowded pubs or parties. A multitude of excuses might be offered which will try the partner to their limit and cause endless anguish and suffering to the shy person.

All too often, though, the shy person can end up in an abusive relationship. They become embroiled with partners who enjoy control. The sufferer is only too pleased to be in a relationship and will accept abusive situations that no other person would accept for fear of having no relationship at all. This is a tragic state of affairs and reflects the lack of self-esteem that so badly needs to be corrected in the shy person.

For a man the problem is even worse as he frequently feels that he has to make the first move in a relationship by asking the girl out. The agony can be too much to bear and consequently the sufferer retreats into his little shell and fails to form the emotionally satisfying relationship that is his natural right.

SOCIALIZING

Socializing is like a game. You need to find your unique selling point. Sit down and decide what your strong points are, then focus on these strong points and guide the conversation to them whenever possible. Firstly, however, you need to listen to the other person to find out what *their* unique points are.

From the time that you first meet someone it really is important to find out about them – for a start, try to establish what their major interests are and see if you can establish some common ground. Once you have opened up and begun to tell them things of interest about yourself they will then enter into the conversation. If necessary, comment on something of interest about what they are wearing, or your surroundings, or the event which you are both attending. Try to find as many common points of interest with the other person as possible.

As we know, and shy people know better than most, social situations can be a nightmare! However, rest assured that you are certainly not alone with this fear. People enjoy having a conversation with somebody who is a good listener. In fact, it is frequently noted by people who like to talk, which is probably 75 per cent of the population, that such-and-such is a very good conversationalist, although in fact that person is simply a very good listener.

Use the techniques taught to you in Chapter 4. These skills will become much easier with practice. Try to socialize with people who have similar interests to yourself. A suggestion I made to one of my patients, that she should do a survey of people and ask them what they did to achieve a good conversation and keep it going, produced absolutely stunning results. People flocked to tell her what made a good conversation and how they were absolutely brilliant conversationalists. She gathered almost enough material for a book.

Focus on where you wish your future to lie – and then *design* your future. Make a decision about current relationships, either enhance them or, if they are abusive, chuck out what is not acceptable. Decide that this relationship will not continue as it is. A lack of focus can lead you to stay in bad situations and in a bad relationship. Without any goals, any aims, or any focus you will just drift through your life. Once you have changed this simple thing and given yourself a focus your life will begin to transform. I guarantee it.

Remember that you are a very unique and special

individual. Recreate your feeling of uniqueness and specialness – and keep reinforcing it, keep telling yourself how special you are. You have one passage through life. This is a unique experience. You were born to live this life; it is a game and you should play it fully. Do not sell yourself short. Stop undervaluing yourself and recognize that this passage through life is a gift – don't allow it to be wasted in an abusive situation.

Frequently, when you suddenly decide to put your foot down, one of two things will happen. The relationship will end and something better will come in its place – you will recreate yourself and decide that the person who is abusing you no longer has a place in your life; or they will respect you to the point where they cease to abuse you.

SCHOOL

If you are being crippled by shyness at school, perhaps, as is often the case, because of bullying by your peers, this should be reported to your parents and to your teacher. Your school should institute a proper bullying policy, and should be supportive in these circumstances.

Perhaps your shyness is due to your not having asserted yourself and not having been able to make many friends. Try to get involved in as many activities at school as possible, thus laying yourself open to making new friends.

If you are an extremely sensitive child who has been bullied at school you may well find it impossible to go to school. This may cross over and become a problem as you start to go to work. Often children, especially girls, go to school and have to have a special friend. This is terribly important and a third child will only intrude. This causes problems if there is an uneven number of quiet children. This leaves an odd one out who may be prone to bullying. You may have stopped going to school. You always want somebody around. Shyness rears its ugly head and you become scared and traumatized, don't want to leave your mother out of fright, and dependence on others grows. You worry about school friends, especially at night and first thing in the morning. Feelings of fear and worry ensue and you imagine the other children talking about you. Panic attacks start, beginning in the stomach. You feel dizzy, shaky, your head swims at the thought of going to school. You fear being left alone by friends, but you don't like being part of a big group. Maybe you feel very left out. Depression results and you want to cry. You may have sleeping problems and disturbed dreams. Eventually you can't make it into school at all. You have panic attacks and stage fright.

Often the school has little or no anti-bullying policy and the troubled children are told just to buck up and that it will toughen them up for life. Unfortunately this very rarely proves to be the case. What often happens instead is that the child simply has even more days off school, gets left more and more behind and is also less able to cope with returning. The child may come up with all sorts of physical symptoms that are psychosomatic simply to avoid going into a horrific situation. There may also be a physical problem making the child feel different – perhaps, Irritable Bowel Syndrome triggered partly by the child's troubled emotional state. This may all be part and parcel of this distressing problem.

BLUSHING

Blushing is a peril of everyday life for some people and, in fact, it can almost *rule* their lives. When you realize that blushing has mastery over you, that it controls you, you need to take control and decide who should be the master. Once you make the switch and recognize the fact that people don't find blushing anything to be ashamed of, you can begin to transform your life – transforming the way that you view blushing can help you do just that. Perhaps it springs from a lack of security, maybe you came from a secure and sheltered place to a place of uncertainty and suddenly you began to feel uncomfortable in social situations or at school. You began to feel a freak. Perhaps, though, you are blowing things out of all proportion. Now you need to put them *in* proportion. Blushing is a throwback from primitive man. Perhaps it is a protective device for when embarrassment and the anger caused by bullying can't be controlled.

One of my patients had this experience. He said he felt like the character in *How to Get Ahead in Advertising*, the Richard E Grant film about a man with two heads. He had been badly bullied at school and told that he would be lucky if he got even one GCSE. That's where the problem began. When he realized his whole future could be at stake if he performed badly in his exams, he panicked and pulled himself together. In fact, he flew through his exams scoring very high marks and is now poised to start training as a lawyer. However, there was always a voice inside him saying he was worthless. Once he began to determine the causes of blushing he steamed ahead and turned the corner.

Blushing is acutely embarrassing to some people, even though it is a natural response of the body. To begin to conquer it, avoid coffee and other stimulants which will aggravate the situation by stimulating your adrenal system. You already know that blushing is something that you will notice and focus on rather than focusing on other people. When people see your discomfort they may make joking remarks about your blushing but try and focus upon the fact that they still continue to speak to you, and want to do so. Draw a conclusion from that and make a mental note that your blushing offends nobody but yourself. Please also follow the exercises contained in this book.

Many people find blushing in other people to be very attractive. I have always been prone to blushing, but fortunately years ago I focused on the fact that it was something others liked about me. Many moons ago, when I was a stewardess for British Airways, I had a relationship with the manager of a hotel in Barbados where the air crew regularly stayed – he asked me out simply because I blushed and he found it so attractive. We dated for quite some time and he never tired of telling me that few girls blushed, which was a shame because he found it very attractive. As is often the case, what *you* may view as a minus point others may see as a positive one or even not notice at all.

PANIC ATTACKS

Panic attacks can strike any of us at any time. They can often be traced back to suppressed childhood trauma and/or controlling or abusive situations in our past. There may have been instances of neglect, punishment or severe criticism that have been suppressed and denied throughout your life and suddenly the subconscious copes in the only way it knows possible – by triggering a panic attack. This naturally ensures that you do not go into an unwanted situation, i.e. something that the subconscious wants to avoid, so is a self-preservation and self-protection mechanism. You may have pains across the chest, palpitations, or even choking sensations.

People are frequently told to pull themselves together if they dare to admit to the outside world they are shy. Shyness can ruin lives. Breaking the self-destructive behaviour of shyness by analysing your thoughts and speech patterns can help you conquer shyness and begin to live your life. Having myself been extremely shy, obese and lacking in self-confidence as a teenager and young adult, I know how difficult it is to overcome this crippling and soul-destroying condition. However, my own learning curve will benefit all who read this book and choose to put into practice the proven methods of my clinic at the London Shyness Centre at the Hale Clinic, and will help them to overcome this condition.

Destructive inner dialogue or faulty self-talk basically comes from the 'stupid' centre of your brain. If you keep telling yourself that you are shy, that other people are looking at you, that you are not good enough to be where you are, then you are not listening to what people around you are saying. What you are probably doing is focusing on what selected people have said to you. The cruellest words and unkindest comments always remain with us and are more powerful than the many kind remarks that are made to us. Alleviating and ending this pattern is achieved simply by focusing on the kind and the positive remarks that people make and very firmly noting that there are more positive remarks made to us than negative remarks.

To consider self-esteem and positive inner dialogue to be self-indulgent and arrogant is a recipe for disaster. As children we are told that to praise ourselves is bad. Parents may be wonderful, kind, generous, special – but the input of our beloved parents can be extraordinarily destructive. Loving yourself and knowing your own self-worth is, in fact, neither self-indulgent nor arrogant. Do not be afraid to recognize your good points and focus on the positive. Not until you can truly love yourself can you also open the doors for the rest of the world to love you too.

CHAPTER 6

The Remedies

HOMEOPATHY

Homeopathy, combined with the techniques outlined in this book, creates an intensely dynamic healing process. Each therapy given in this book is powerful in its own right, but by integrating the therapies, the healing process is more effective and the shy person can progress more rapidly to a life devoid of irrational fear. Changing the way people view the world and themselves will empower each one of them.

WHAT IS HOMEOPATHY?

Homeopathy is a complete system of medicine that aims to promote natural health by reinforcing the body's own healing powers. Conventional medicine uses drugs which block the body's own responses to a condition and which suppress the elimination of toxins, disrupting the body's natural balance. Homeopathy, by contrast, works by correcting energy imbalances: minute doses of substances which are similar to the condition are used to 'match' the energy of the illness, thereby stimulating the body's own healing energy.

Homeopathy is a safe, non-toxic treatment that has no side-effects. Improvement is fast, yet gentle, as remedies bring the body into balance, correcting its level of amino acids and cell salts, eliminating allergens and toxins and restoring the body's own intelligent healing system. Homeopathy also treats the patient on an emotional as well as physical level: everyone is unique and, as such, requires an individual remedy.

Homeopathy aims to promote an enhanced pattern of health by reinforcing the body's own healing ability. Each individual will respond differently to the remedy given. The remedies boost the body's own healing power and therefore there can be no prior knowledge as to how each individual will react to the remedies given.

There are many different methods of prescribing homeo-pathy. There is single-remedy prescribing, practised by many lay homeopaths and also by many medical homeopaths. Complex homeopathy, as practised by lay homeopaths and doctors and used widely on the Continent, is now a growing art in this country, as is bio-energetic testing, which has been termed 21st-century medicine. And finally there are the flower remedies, such as the Bach Flower Remedies, Bailey Flower Essences, the Bush Flower Remedies and the Californian Flower Remedies.

Many emotional problems are deeply ingrained and may have caused the physical problem that the sufferer is now struggling with. Deep-seated and unexpressed anger, suppressed grief, or traumatic occurrences that have not been dealt with, are often the causal factor in a physical ailment. For example, many cancer sufferers are 'nice people'! They suppress their anger and fail to assert themselves. The body–mind relationship used to be clearly understood by family doctors at the turn of the century, but now people are viewed as disconnected parts and the body's reaction to denied emotion is ignored.

Anger also is not acceptable in our society. Assertiveness is only now beginning to be taught. People have little sense of loving self. Self-nurturing is seen as indulgent and selfish. It is hardly surprising that the body succumbs to sickness.

Homeopathy can be used either for acute prescribing or for chronic longer term prescribing. In acute prescribing homeopathy is astoundingly fast. In chronic prescribing it takes longer but effects a lasting and permanent cure.

HOW DOES HOMEOPATHY WORK?

Homeopathy is basically a healing process using natural remedies in minute quantities that have been processed in such a way that there is virtually nothing left of the original substance. As you go to a higher potency an energy is left as a sort of genetic fingerprint. The remedy is chosen to match the energy level on which a person is vibrating at any given time, taking into account the emotional, the physical and the general state of the person.

IS HOMEOPATHY SAFE?

The dilution process through which homeopathic remedies pass means that homeopathic remedies are completely safe, non-addictive and non-toxic. There are no unwanted side-effects, even for children, pregnant women and babies. Even though the original substances may be toxic the high dilution rate ensures that the danger of toxicity is eliminated.

IS HOMEOPATHY EFFECTIVE?

It has been proven to be effective and is used to treat millions of people worldwide.

IS HOMEOPATHY OFFICIALLY RECOGNIZED?

Yes, it is recognized by Acts of Parliament and is practised by many doctors who are conventionally trained in medicine. It has been used by many members of the Royal Family for six generations.

Homeopathy has often been likened to a placebo response. However, this has now been disproved. It is widely used in the UK, Europe, and both North and South America. It is also used for animals and this, along with other research, disproves the myth that it is all in the mind.

WHEN SHOULD I SEE A QUALIFIED HOMEOPATH?

When you have a long-standing or chronic condition. Simple First Aid or minor ailments can be self-treated. Many complex homeopathic packs are aimed specifically at such conditions as insomnia, hay fever, headaches, stress, nervous conditions, depression etc. If you take a remedy and only achieve partial relief then consult a qualified homeopath who can prescribe more precisely.

COMPLEX HOMEOPATHY

Complex homeopathy is a method of combining homeopathic remedies using different potencies. It incorporates the theory of organ drainage according to which various organs such as the liver and kidneys are drained and cleansed. The potencies range from low to high and a perfect example of complex homeopathy can be seen when one looks at the Nelsons insomnia or hayfever preparations available in Boots the Chemist. These are not single remedies but many different remedies. Many people may be treated effectively simply by purchasing a homeopathic formula that combines many of the best known homeopathic remedies for a specific ailment; one is sure to hit its mark. This is not perfect prescribing but it empowers the general public to self-treat safely and effectively.

HOMEOPATHIC REMEDIES

Choose the section which describes your condition fully. Then check each of the listed remedies at the back in the Materia Medica for the one that most appropriately fits your symptoms then check the potency and frequency.

AFRAID OF BEING HUMILIATED
LYCOPODIUM
NATRUM MURIATICUM
STAPHYSAGRIA

AFRAID OF REJECTION
See Rejection–Fear of

ANGER
ACONITE
BELLADONNA
NUX VOMICA
STAPHYSAGRIA
WILLOW (BACH FLOWER REMEDY)

ANXIETY
ARGENTUM NITRICUM
ARSENICUM
HYOSCYAMUS
LYCOPODIUM
PHOSPHORUS
NATRACALM (BODY DYNAMICS)

APPREHENSION
ACONITE
GELSEMIUM
BELLADONNA

BLUSHING
BELLADONNA
LYCOPODIUM

PULSATILLA
SULPHUR

DEPRESSION AND DESPAIR
ANACARDIUM
LIFELIGHTS (BODY DYNAMICS)
ARSENICUM
CALCAREA CARBONICA
LYCOPODIUM
NATRUM MUR
NUX VOMICA
PULSATILLA
STAPHISAGRIA
SULPHUR

FEAR OF PUBLIC SPEAKING
LYCOPODIUM

FEAR SOMETHING WILL HAPPEN
CAUSTICUM
NUX VOMICA
PHOSPHORUS
TUBERCULINUM
NATRACALM (BODY DYNAMICS)

FEAR OF FAILURE
ARGENTUM NITRICUM
ARNICA
CARCINOCIN
LARCH (BACH FLOWER REMEDY)
GELSEMIUM
LYCOPODIUM
NUX VOMICA
PHOSPHORUS

FEAR AND ANXIETY
ACONITE
ARGENTUM NITRICUM

LARCH (BACH FLOWER REMEDY)
GELSEMIUM
PHOSPHORUS
PULSATILLA
NATRACALM (BODY DYNAMICS)
CERATO (BACH FLOWER REMEDY)

FEAR OF FAILING EXAMS
ANACARDIUM
ARGENTUM NITRICUM
CARCINOCIN
GELSEMIUM
LYCOPODIUM
NATRACALM (BODY DYNAMICS)

FEAR OF MEETINGS
ARGENTUM NITRICUM
VALERIANA
NATRACALM (BODY DYNAMICS)

LACK OF SELF ESTEEM
ANACARDIUM
CARCINOCIN
GELSEMIUM
LYCOPODIUM
MEDORRHINUM
NATRUM MURIATICUM
NUX VOMICA
PHOSPHORUS
LARCH (BACH FLOWER REMEDY)
PULSATILLA
STAPHYSAGRIA
SYPHILLINUM
THUJA
CERATO (BACH FLOWER REMEDY)

PANIC ATTACKS
ACONITE
ARGENTUM NITRICUM

ARSENICUM ALBUM
GELSEMIUM
KALI ARSENICUM
LYCOPODIUM
NATRACALM (BODY DYNAMICS)
LAVENDER OIL
PHOSPHORUS
RESCUE REMEDY (BACH FLOWER REMEDIES)
VALERIANA

PROCRASTINATION
HORNBEAM (BACH FLOWER REMEDY)
LARCH (BACH FLOWER REMEDY)
NATRUM MURIATICUM

REJECTION – FEAR OF
GENTIAN (BACH FLOWER REMEDIES)
LARCH (BACH FLOWER REMEDIES)

SEXUAL FEARS
ARGENTUM NITRICUM
LYCOPODIUM
PULSATILLA
SULPHUR

MATERIA MEDICA (OR REMEDY PICTURES)

Check this section for each of the remedies mentioned and choose the remedy that seems to fit you. You won't have all of the symptoms mentioned but if you find a striking resemblance, ie, you suffer from panic attacks with palpitations especially before an ordeal, then choose aconite.

SYMPTOMS
Symptoms of the same ailment are quite often radically different in two different people. When deciding on the

most appropriate remedy look at the symptoms listed under each remedy and decide which most closely fits you. For example, one person with claustrophobia may have diarrhoea or a migraine from the anxiety of going into a crowded place. They want to be in the cool fresh air. This person would take argentum nitricum.

Another person who also has a fear of enclosed places but may cry very easily and doesn't drink much liquid, is generally a thirstless person. Pulsatilla would be an appropriate remedy for this person. Both have claustrophobia but each has different symptoms.

TREATMENT
It is important that you self-treat using homeopathic remedies only until you are able to find a qualified practitioner to help you. You can use the above remedies in either 6c or 30c potency in acute and emergency situations, or just to get you out of the house. However the problem will be deep and underlying and you deserve help. To find a qualified practitioner *see* page 87.

ACONITE
Fear of crowds. Great anxiety, agonizing fear and restlessness. Sudden panic, palpitations. Shock. Nervous and anxious state, dread of ordeals. Fear of death or injury. Fear of public places because there is a fear that death or injury is inevitable. Dreadful foreboding. Prediction of time of death. Claustrophobia, panic attacks, agoraphobia, fear of driving, fear of doctors, dentists, fear of aeroplanes.

This remedy can be taken in 30c potency up to 3 times a day for two or three days. Also take just before going into a difficult situation.

ANACARDIUM
Loss of will and cannot control vocabulary. Thinking becomes difficult, the memory weak. Lacking in self-confidence. This person may have been put down or possibly beaten. There is much suppressed anger. Because

of his hate he desires revenge. He may suffer from a fear of failing exams.

This remedy should be taken three times a day for one day. Repeat this one day a week for a month.

ARGENTUM NITRICUM (ARG NIT)

Anticipation, anxiety and fear, diarrhoea when anxious. Fear may cause nervous hysteria. Fear of crowds. Tormented by irrational fears and strange ideas. Timid and anxious person. May have a migraine with anticipation. Better in the cool fresh air and for motion. Worse for worry and mental strain. Fears heights, and suffers vertigo. Fears high buildings, even the sight of high buildings makes him giddy. Seems as if the houses on both sides of the street would crush him. Exam nerves. Fears death. Apprehensive and lacking in self-confidence. Stage fright. Claustrophobia, panic attacks, fear of being alone, agoraphobia, fear of failure, and failing exams. Fear of driving, doctors, dentists, and aeroplanes.

This remedy can be taken in 30c potency up to 3 times a day for two or three days. Also take just before going into a difficult situation.

ARNICA

This remedy is the trauma remedy. Not only physical trauma, but bruised feelings and emotional trauma, that of loss, grief or shock. This person is scared when someone approaches her. Greatly fears crowds and public places. Also has fears at night and on waking. She may suffer from agoraphobia, and fear of failure.

This remedy should be taken three times a day for one day. Repeat this one day a week for a month.

ARSENICUM ALBUM

Scared of robbers and of death. Phobic. Nervous and anxious and restless in the extreme. Cannot bear to be alone. Irrational fears. Fear of being alone in case she does herself bodily harm. Incredibly neat and tidy. Suffers from panic attacks, fear of being alone, fear of medicine, fear of homosexuality, obsessive compulsive disorders.

This remedy should be taken twice a day for one day. Repeat this one day a week for a month.

BELLADONNA
Redness, sudden blushing, shyness with restless behaviour and overactivity. Panic, anxiety over social events, nightmares. Twitching and convulsive movements. Restless sleep. Fear and a dry mouth.

This remedy should be taken three times a day for one day. Repeat this one day a week for a month.

CALCAREA CARBONICA (CALC CARB)
Apprehensive, prefers to stay at home. An overwhelmed mental state due to worry. Fears disaster. Anxiety with palpitations. Obstinate and irritable. Melancholic. Thinks people are looking at him. May suffer from agoraphobia and fear of driving, animals, spiders, doctors, hospitals, dentists, heights and aeroplanes.

This remedy should be taken three times a day for one day. Repeat this one day a week for a month.

CARCINOCIN
Fearful of the future. A 'nice' person who has suppressed her anger. Fitting in with everyone else, she lacks self-esteem. When upset can't communicate it to others. Fear is often felt in the pit of the stomach. May be fastidious. There may be chronic insomnia. May suffer from fear of failure, fear of failing exams, and obsessive compulsive disorders.

This remedy should be taken three times a day for one day. Repeat this one day a week for a month.

CAUSTICUM
Sympathetic, worries about others even when fearful. Always prefers cold drinks. Anxious. Suffers from the fear that something might happen.

This remedy should be taken twice a day for one day. Repeat this one day a week for a month.

CERATO
Fear of failure, depends on others for advice, inability to trust one's own judgement. Take as directed on the bottle.

GELSEMIUM
This person lacks confidence, feels frail and weak. He develops hypochondria when feeling vulnerable. States of confusion. This person wants to be held. Tremors or twitching of single muscle. Dazed states may occur. May be emotional and fearful. Suffering the ill effects of fright. Feelings of dread.

This person wishes to be quiet and left alone. Dullness of the intellect. He may experience dizziness and go weak at the knees. There might be diarrhoea or incontinence, alternatively he might need to pass copious quantities of urine. Shakes with fright. A tendency to fly into a panic. School phobia. Flies into a panic especially with fear of insects or spiders. May suffer from agoraphobia or have fear of failure, fear of failing exams. This might be a person who fears doctors, hospitals or dentists. A fear of heights may be one of the fears.

This remedy should be taken twice a day for one day. Repeat this one day a week for a month.

GENTIAN
Discouraged – fears rejection. Fear of failure. Unable to move on.

Take as directed on the bottle.

HORNBEAM (BACH FLOWER REMEDY)
Lack of energy due to emotional resilience to work. Take as directed on the bottle.

HYOSCYAMUS
Nervous and irritable, this person is easily excitable. Fearful of being alone in case she is pursued. Also has a fear

of being poisoned. Afraid of everyone. Prone to nervous twitchings of the muscles. Incredibly suspicious and jealous. The biggest fear is of being alone.

This remedy should be taken twice a day for one day. Repeat this one day a week for a month.

KALI-ARSENICUM
Sudden noise throws the body into a tremor, therefore suffers panic attacks.

This remedy should be taken three times a day for one day. Repeat this one day a week for a month.

LARCH (BACH FLOWER REMEDY)
Delaying due to fear of failure or lack of self-esteem. Fears judgement by others.

Take as directed on the bottle.

LAVENDER OIL
Frayed nerves, panic attacks and fear. Invokes calmness, tendency to be highly strung.

Take as directed on the bottle.

LIFELIGHTS (BODY DYNAMICS)
Depression and nervousness are the key to this combination pack. Fears of impoverished emotional states, feelings of lack yet hopeful of recovery. Feelings of rejection, loathing of life yet aversion to suicide. Hopeless and melancholic.

Take as directed on the bottle.

LYCOPODIUM
Indecision, timidity and a lack of self-confidence and poor self-esteem. This person often feels apprehensive. Fears being alone. Dependent on others, likes to know someone is in the other room.

Melancholy, afraid to be alone. Better for motion and warm food and drink. Suffers from anticipation, a fear of undertaking anything new, yet things he does undertake he accomplishes with ease. May suffer from a weak memory, possibly have dyslexia, or brain fag. May have a fear of meeting new people. May have a fear of public speaking, fear of being alone, agoraphobia, fear of failure, a fear of failing exams, social fears such as a fear of being humiliated and a fear of impotence.

This remedy should be taken three times a day for one day. Repeat this one day a week for a month.

MEDORRHINUM
Great feelings of sadness, tearfulness. Fears that she will never recover, fears that she is going insane. Time passes slowly. Things seem strange. She feels far off. Brain fag, a loss of concentration. This person keeps repeating things because of poor concentration and poor memory. Much worse during the day; she is a night person. May have a tendency towards drugs, sex and rock and roll. This is a remedy for obsessive compulsive disorders.

This remedy should be taken three times a day for one day. Repeat this one day a week for a month.

NATRACALM (BODY DYNAMICS)
This person is nervous, full of fear. Feels that he needs a sedative. Unable to concentrate, may be confused, restless at night and unable to sleep. Stressed to the extreme, and unable to relax.

Take as directed on the bottle.

NATRUM MURIATICUM (NAT MUR)
Generally dislikes company. Hates consolation. Retreats behind an emotional and physical wall, wanting to be left alone. Wants to be alone to cry. Dislikes sympathy. Fears relationships. Fears being rejected so is anxious. Out of fear does safe things. Depressed and introverted. Dwells on unpleasant past memories. Irritable. Fear of being rejected or hurt emotionally. May have awkward speed patterns that make it difficult to socialize. May be clumsy. Fears narrow places. Claustrophobia, agoraphobia, fear of spiders, hospitals and doctors. May suffer from social fears such as

the fear of being humiliated. May suffer fear of heights, and consequently a fear of aeroplanes. May also suffer from obsessive compulsive disorders. Weakness and no energy. Defensive and rigid. Mood swings common. Ill effects of grief or anger.

This remedy should be taken three times a day for one day. Repeat this one day a week for a month.

NUX VOMICA
This person is irritable, ambitious and hard working. Gets nervous and excited. Angry, impatient, and explosive. Type A personalities. Likes stimulants, coffee, alcohol. Hates consolation. Fears that something will happen. Suffers fear of failure. May have a fear of blood. Also may suffer from obsessive compulsive disorders.

This remedy should be taken three times a day for one day. Repeat this one day a week for a month.

PHOSPHORUS
Incredibly imaginative. Fears may concern twilight, thunderstorms and lightning. Fears that something will creep out of the corner. Fears about the future. Easily startled. May have energy and enthusiasm totally dissipated by unpleasant happenings. Constantly needs reassurance. Absolutely convinced of impending loss or failure. Scared of nightmares. Nervous, weak and delicate. Emotion leaves this person feeling wiped out, as does mental fatigue. Symptoms will be worse at twilight. Anger brings on attack. Anxious and wanting sympathy. The fears and conditions he suffers range from panic attacks to the fear of being alone. Fears that something will happen, fear of failure and a fear of doctors and hospitals.

This remedy should be taken three times a day for one day. Repeat this one day a week for a month.

PULSATILLA
This person may be quite timid, mild, emotional, moody and tearful. Always feels better for getting out into the

open air. Her symptoms feel better for gentle motion. Symptoms tend to shift about the body. Everything is changeable. Quite thirstless. Prone to panic attacks, lack of self-esteem and claustrophobia. May also suffer from obsessive compulsive disorders.

This remedy should be taken three times a day for one day. Repeat this one day a week for a month.

RESCUE REMEDY (BACH FLOWER REMEDY)
Fear, shock, panic attacks, frayed nerves.

Take as directed on the bottle.

STAPHYSAGRIA
Incredibly sensitive and nervous. Easily hurt by people saying the slightest thing. Anger and insults will make this person ill. There is sometimes a history of abuse, verbal, physical or sexual. Anger is suppressed. Always tries to make peace, suppressing anger out of fear. Has a poor self-image and feels worthless. Often shy and apologetic. Has no way of asserting himself. There is often a history of humiliation. Depression. Feelings of injustice which are suppressed. Fear of heights, and a social fear of being humiliated. May also suffer from obsessive compulsive disorders.

This remedy should be taken three times a day for one day. Repeat this one day a week for a month.

SULPHUR
Severe problems with sharing and closeness. Severely depressed to the point of not caring about anything. Confused about feelings. Untidiness is a theme that is both physical and emotional – will inevitably have knock-on effects on confidence. Feet burn and need to be stuck out of the bed at night. Forgetful, irritable and depressed.

This remedy should be taken three times a day for one day. Repeat this one day a week for a month.

SYPHILINUM

May suffer night fears and fears of insanity. Feelings of hopelessness. Extremely restless, waking up feeling totally wiped out in the morning. Far away feelings are common. Compulsive behaviour may be apparent. This person is antisocial at times. Poor concentration and loss of memory. Compulsion to wash hands. Obsessive compulsive disorders.

This remedy should be taken three times a day for one day. Repeat this one day a week for a month.

THUJA

Fixed ideas in a hurried and bad-tempered person. Symptoms are much worse at night in bed. Fears that someone is following him. Gradually he may become very critical and develop a loathing of life. Fear makes this person feel he can predict his time of death. Suffers insomnia and sees things when eyes are closed. May have sexual fears concerning homosexuality. Often suffers from obsessive compulsive disorders.

This remedy should be taken three times a day for one day. Repeat this one day a week for a month.

TUBERCULINUM

This person has intense fatigue but constantly wants changes. May be melancholic and depressed. Has a kind of inner yearning. Restless and irritable but with a seeking for spiritual truth. Romantic. Dissatisfied, always seeking changes. Burning the candle at both ends, lives life to the full. May have a loathing for cats and dogs.

This person is prone to colds that end with diarrhoea. She is hopeless and anxious. Her fears centre around the fear that something will happen.

This remedy should be taken three times a day for one day. Repeat this one day a week for a month.

VALERIANA

This person suffers from hysteria and is nervous. Over-sensitive and irritable. Insomnia is marked. Feels dreadful on waking.

This remedy should be taken three times a day for one day. Repeat this one day a week for a month.

VISCUM ALBUM
Restless and nervous. There may be apathy or sadness, dwelling on past events. Obsessive dwelling on one thought or one unpleasant occurrence. Fear of telephones.

This remedy should be taken three times a day for one day. Repeat this one day a week for a month.

WILLOW (BACH FLOWER REMEDY)
Anger deeply held. Bitterness and resentment. Unable to forgive and move on. Fears and feelings of rejection.

Take as directed on the bottle.

Sanjeevini – Healing with Prayers

Worship is not a uniform to be put on and off at stated hours of the day. Render every thought into a flower, worthy to be held in His Fingers; render every deed into a fruit, full of the sweet juice of love, fit to be placed in His Hand; render every tear holy and pure, fit to wash His Feet

Bhagawan Sri Sathya Sai Baba

SANATHANA SAI SANJEEVINI

A Gift of Love

'Prayers can move mountains.' This is a teaching which is common to all religions. Faith can move mountains and a prayer seeking help from your God will always bring a response.

Sanjeevini is a system of prayers to God that has been introduced to healers quite recently. Since that time those healers have grown in numbers, scope and power. This Sanjeevini organization has grown in leaps and bounds. Healers from all over the world are now adding healing by prayer to their other therapies. In my practice I teach my patients how to take this method into their own home and to enhance their own healing.

The Sanjeevinis are obviously an answer to our prayers. The system is simple, easy to use and far-reaching. The healers using the Sanjeevini system come from all over the world, from all faiths and all religions. Their feedback to the Sanjeevini organization is that the results are 'astonishing', 'amazing', 'instantaneous', and 'miraculous'.

The Sanjeevinis are highly focused prayers. How they work defies explanation on the physical level. The healers know that it is not they who are healing – it is God. The Sanjeevinis, in their true form, are a gift of love from God. PRAYERS CAN MOVE MOUNTAINS.

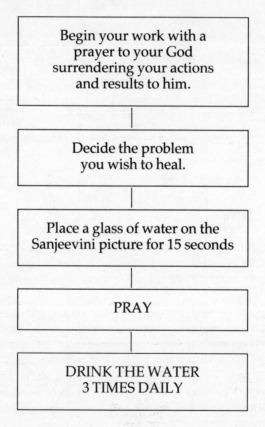

Note 1: While preparing the Sanjeevinis, chanting your favourite prayers or affirmation from any religion or faith would further enhance the value of the Sanjeevinis, besides

Sanathana Sai SAFE (scars of Abuse, Fears Eradication) Sanjeevini 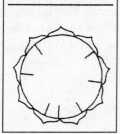	Sanathana Sai Sleep Sanjeevini 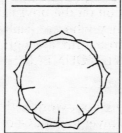	Sanathana Sai Shakthip Sanjeevini 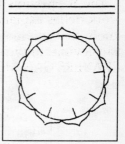
Sanathana Sai Shanthi Sanjeevini 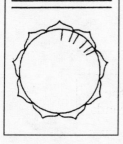	Sanathana Sai Thought Management Sanjeevini 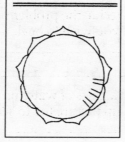	Sanathana Sai Nervous System Sanjeevini 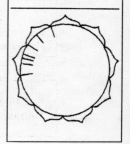
Sanathana Sai Shock Sanjeevini 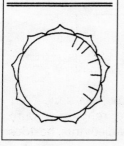	Sanathana Sai Whole Body Sanjeevini 	Sanathana Sai Mind Sanjeevini 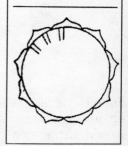

purifying the healer at the same time. Visualizing your favourite deity helps concentration.

Note 2: It is perfectly all right to keep the glass on the relevant Sanjeevini Card for more than 15 seconds.

For your own unique and powerful remedy for shyness, repeat the above procedure placing the glass on each picture in succession until you finally come to the Whole Body card.

CAUTION: Under no circumstances must anyone be asked to discontinue any allopathic or other medicines they are taking. These Sanjeevinis do not disturb the action of these medicines. Please remember that the Sanjeevinis are focused prayer and can do no harm. At a subtler level, a deeper healing will be effected by the Sanjeevinis through the awakening of the body's own healing power.

Anger, malice, greed, envy – all these are obstacles in the path of love and co-operation. They lower man from the Divine to the animal level. Bear with others in patience and understanding; practice 'sahan' and sympathy. Try to discover point of contact, not of conflict. Spread brotherliness and deepen kindness through knowledge. Then life becomes worthwhile, without fail.

Bhagawan Sri Sathya Sai

Useful Addresses

HOMEOPATHIC REMEDIES

Ainsworths Pharmacy
38 New Cavendish Street
London
W1M 7LH
England

Tel: 0171 935 5330

Body Dynamics
New Vistas Healthcare
Plassey Technological Park
Limerick, Ireland

Tel: 00353 61 334455
Fax: 00353 61 331515

Helios Homoeopathic
Pharmacy
97 Camden Road
Tunbridge Wells
Kent TN1 2QR
England

Tel: 01892 537254/536393

Nelsons Homoeopathic
Pharmacy
73 Duke Street
London W1M 6BY
England

Tel: 0171 629 3118

SHYNESS CLINIC

The London Shyness Centre
The Hale Clinic
7 Park Crescent
London W1N 3HE
England

Tel: 0171 631 0156
Fax: 0171 323 1693

HOMOEOPATHIC TRAINING

Practical College of
Homoeopathy
422 Hackney Road
London E2 7SY
England

Tel: 0171 613 5468

BIO-ENERGETIC TESTING

The London Bio-Dynamics
Centre
The Hale Clinic
7 Park Crescent
London
W1N 3HE
England

Tel: 0171 289 2882
Fax: 0171 289 4317

BULLYING ADVICE

Kidscape
152 Buckingham Palace Road
London
SW1W 9TR
England

Tel: 0171 730 3300

REGISTERS OF HOMEOPATHIC PRACTITIONERS

UKHMA
United Kingdom
Homoeopathic Medical Assn
6 Livingstone Road
Gravesend
Kent
DA12 5DZ
England

Tel: 01474 560336

International Foundation of
Homeopathy
2366 East Lake Avenue East
301
Seattle
WA 98102
USA

Tel/Fax: 011 206 3248230

American Institute of
Homeopathic Medicine
(includes doctors, dentists,
vets)
925 East 17th Avenue
Denver
CO 80218-1407
USA

Tel: 303 898 5477

National Centre for
Homeopathy
801 North Fairfax Street
Suit 306 Alexandria
VA 22314
USA

Tel: 703 548 7790
Fax: 703 548 7792

NLP ASSOCIATIONS

ANLP
Association of Neuro
Linguistic Programming
PO Box 78
Stourbridge
West Midlands
DY8 2YP

Tel: 01384 443935

NLP TRAINERS

PACE Ltd
86 Southill Park
London
NW3 2SM
England

Tel: 0171 794 0960

John Grinder
Quantum Lea Incorporated
PO Box 67359
Scotta Valley
California 95067
USA

Fax: 408 457 2834

NLP Comprehensive
5695 Yukon Street
Arvada
Colorado 80002
USA

Tel: 800 233 1657
Fax: 303 442 1102

Lifelong Learning Ltd
55 Blomfield Road
London
W9 2PD

Tel: 0171 289 2882
Fax: 0171 289 4317

WHOLISTIC NLP CLINIC AND TRAINING

The Ravenscroft Centre
6 Ravenscroft Avenue
London
NW11 0RY
England

Tel: 0181 455 3743
Fax: 0181 201 8319

MEMBERS OF ANLP IN AUSTRALIA

Glen Farrell
15 Albert Avenue
Suite 152
Broad Beach
Queensland 4218
Australia

Tel: 0 755 349120

Helena Johansen
112–118 Carbrooke Road
Cornubia
Queensland 4130
Australia

Tel: 073 287 6599

Further Reading

Andreas, Connirae, Andreas, Steve, *Heart of the Mind*, Real People Press, 1989

Coelho, Paulo, *The Alchemist*, Thorsons, 1993

Field, Lynda, *Creating Self-Esteem*, Element Books, 1993

Grant, Wendy, *Dare!*, Element Books, 1996

Hay, Louise, *You Can Heal Your Life*, Eden Grove, 1988

Jeffers, S, *Feel The Fear and Do It Anyway*, Arrow

Lee, Kenneth & McKellar, *I Want To be Good*, Chance In Time Press, 1997

Lindenfield, G, *Super Confidence*, Thorsons, 1989

Markham, Ursula, *Creating A Positive Self Image*, Element Books, 1995

Peiffer, Vera, *Positively Fearless*, Element Books, 1995

Robbins, Anthony, *Awaken The Giant Within*, Simon & Schuster, 1992

Syer, S & Connolly, *Think To Win*, Simon & Schuster, 1991

Index